ORIGINAL
JAGUAR XK

ORIGINAL
JAGUAR XK

Philip Porter
Photography by Tim Andrew
Edited by Mark Hughes

BAY
VIEW
BOOKS

Published 1988 by
Bay View Books Ltd
13a Bridgeland Street
Bideford
Devon EX39 2QE

Reprinted 1990

© Copyright 1988
Bay View Books Ltd

Designed by Bruce Aiken
Typeset by Lens Typesetting
Bideford

ISBN 1-870979-05-2

Printed in Hong Kong

Contents

Introduction

I have always thought that the maxim 'each to his own' should apply to cars, including Jaguar XKs. If a proud owner wants to paint his car orange with alternate purple stripes and pink spots, that is his decision. The thought does not appeal to me, but it is neither for me nor anyone else to tell him that he's wrong.

Most people, however, wish to own an XK that is 'as original' – some more fanatically than others. Ideally, of course, one would own a car that actually is original, exactly as it was when it left the factory, but the ravages of time, salted roads, corrosion and undiscriminating previous owners mean that very few cars are totally original, whatever may be claimed.

The aim of most owners is to recreate their cars as they were when first made. Depending on your viewpoint, it is either obsessive to want to know whether your car's wing piping should be made of leather cloth or PVC – this is just one point which produces intense disagreement! – or part of the fun of ownership. Some of us will be more concerned about these detailed aspects than others. Of one thing there is no doubt: the subject of originality is a minefield. It is also a continuing debate, but as time passes more facts are established.

In order to try to distinguish fact from fiction, we sought out and photographed in detail no fewer than 10 excellent cars. As it was the intention of this book to be photographically appealing as well as informative we engaged Tim Andrew, one of Britain's top motoring photographers, to spend a week capturing every aspect of these cars in delightful settings. The results speak for themselves. The lenses of his Nikons have peered into, under and over all manner of objects – even through the branches of an apple tree in which he precariously balanced for the cover shot – to record these XKs in delicious detail. This obliging tree and many of the views seen between these covers are to be found at Prescott hillclimb in Gloucestershire.

Having photographed these carefully selected cars, we had to be sure that they would satisfy the eagle eye of the expert reader. I can state without fear of contradiction that no-one is an expert on *every* aspect of *every* XK. So it was that I assembled a forum of people with unrivalled experience in the field of XKs to examine all the photographs, offering what criticisms they could. It led to much intriguing debate.

Our panel of experts was distinguished. Aubrey Finburgh of Classic Autos has specialised in every aspect of XK120s for over 20 years, including restoration to genuinely high standards, panel work and parts. Richard Woodley is a most knowledgeable enthusiast who has owned several superb XKs for many years, and organised and judged many concours events. John Pearson has owned XKs, raced them, rebuilt them and sold them for umpteen years. Bob Smith of RS Panels is one of the top builders of car bodies and restorers in Britain. Mick Turley of Suffolk & Turley, ex-factory trimmers *par excellence*, has an enviable reputation in his field. David Cottingham of DK Engineering has bought and sold XKs over a long period, raced them, restored them and now owns a particularly famous one. Ian Macleod, and his son Bruce, of Contour Autocraft spend all their time building panels and complete bodies for XKs, struggling to meet the demand. John Hedges is a great enthusiast who has owned several examples for a long time, and has been particularly active in organising Jaguar events at Beaulieu over the years. Apart from having been until recently Chairman of the XK Register of the Jaguar Drivers Club, John Bridcutt puts us all to shame by using his XK140 as everyday transport. To all these experts I must offer my sincere thanks for their invaluable assistance.

With nearly 200 years of collective XK experience, this panel set about the photographs. We quickly discovered that no car is perfect, and so the captions inevitably include some qualifications. To complement this six-hour 'think-tank' I also spent time at Jaguar researching old records. With the generous help of Ian Luckett, who looks after the archives and has supplied countless owners with details of their cars, I dug deep into yellowing, curling pages.

This brought home to me the myriad minor changes that have been made since the late forties. It would take several volumes to describe every alteration of nut and bolt, every addition or deletion of a washer. However, I finally found, with Ian's assistance, the answer to the wing piping conundrum!

While making qualifications, it is important to stress that a customer could order any colour and combination of paintwork and trim that he desired, so there will always be exceptions. What I have tried to do is establish the rule. In order to further my knowledge, I read through much published correspondence on the subject from the last 10 years, and I am therefore grateful to all those who have made their contributions over this period. The subject has certainly stimulated much lively debate.

I must thank the owners of the cars – or should I say victims? – who kindly and bravely allowed the objects of their love to be photographed for this book. I hope that they will take any very minor criticisms of their lovely cars in the spirit

in which they are meant. We have attempted to be super-critical on the subject of originality, and sincerely hope that in doing so we haven't offended anyone's pride.

Vic Gill (silver 120 OTS), Stuart Holden (green 120 OTS), Michael and Peter Sargent (120 FHC), Pieter Zwakman (120 DHC), Barrie Williams (140 DHC), Alan Minchin (140 OTS), John Ruff (140 FHC), Chris Fletcher (150 FHC), Peter Walker (150 OTS) and John Schofield (150 DHC) gave their time most generously. The exceptional photographs are a fine tribute to their splendid cars. We are fortunate to be able to use Prescott as our venue, and would like to express our gratitude to Geoffrey and Sue Ward of the Bugatti Owners Club for giving us every assistance with such exceptional courtesy.

My task of sorting out parts availability and interchangeability was greatly eased by Trevor Scott-Worthington of Coventry Auto Components and his comprehensive catalogue of re-manufactured items.

On a personal note, I should like to thank the publisher, Charles Herridge, for asking me to write such a challenging and terrifying book, and the series editor, my very good friend Mark Hughes for much advice and assistance, and for operating the slide projector for six hours!

The aim of *Original Jaguar XK* is to share the pleasures of these cars and to assist those who wish to recreate their cars as they left the factory. The aim is not to encourage a breed of mollycoddled XKs taken to concours d'elegance events on trailers. I feel strongly that these cars were designed to be driven enthusiastically, and therein lies the real pleasure of XK ownership. Undoubtedly that pleasure is heightened for many of us if the car is 'as original'.

XK Past and Present

When it was launched in 1948, the Jaguar XK120 was unique. Announced at the Earls Court Motor Show, it was, to use an over-worked expression, an 'overnight sensation'. The reasons were simple.

The new Jaguar sports car brought racing car performance to the road, yet it did so with a level of comfort and sophistication unknown in such a vehicle. It was offered at an extraordinarily low price, and it was endowed with a body of lasting beauty.

The car was intended for limited production only to try out Jaguar's new twin overhead camshaft engine, designated during design and development by the initials 'XK'. It was destined for a new range of large saloons (sedans) which were of far more commercial importance to the company. As a bonus, it was thought, the sports car might bring a little publicity to Jaguar and enhance the image of the company's products.

Previously the twin overhead camshaft layout had been considered too complex and impractical for production. Although engines of this design can be traced back a good way, they were generally associated with racing cars or very limited production hand-built high performance cars. As a result of intelligent engineering, and a fair amount of courage, Jaguar was able to build such an engine and prove it to be a practical proposition.

In its original form, the engine gave 160bhp, sufficient to endow the XK120 with a top speed to match its name and exceptional acceleration. The car was the fastest in production in the world, but equally its other great quality was a smoothness and docility that contrasted vividly with this stupendous performance. The XK120 had a Jekyll and Hyde character: it could be raced successfully or it could potter through New York traffic.

As the XK120's chassis was 'borrowed' in cut-down form from the contemporary Jaguar saloon, it was designed for a heavier car. This 'over-engineering' gave the new car a torsional stiffness that was uncommon in a sports car. The result in practical terms was that its ride was far superior to rivals, and excellent independent front suspension gave admirable roadholding and comfort.

At £1263 (including purchase tax), the exciting new XK120 was amazing value for money, bringing high performance within the reach of far more people. One no longer needed to be a millionaire to enjoy such a car, although one probably still looked it.

This was William Lyons' (he was knighted in 1956) great secret. Pre-war his cars looked like Bentleys without the pedigree and performance, yet they cost a fraction of the price. Lyons understood style and packaging, and had a rare – perhaps unique – ability to create body styles himself. There is no better example of his brilliance than the XK120.

Previously Lyons had been heavily influenced by styles of the period, but for his new sports car he applied more adventurous thinking. True, one can see elements of Bugatti influence, and perhaps suggestions of the Mille Miglia BMW 328, but Lyons created a shape that took everyone's breath away in 1948.

It has stood the test of time. Today the XK is rightly revered as an automotive landmark and an exciting machine. The earlier XKs enjoyed considerable success in national and international racing, rallying and record breaking, a pedigree which can only enhance their appeal today.

The pioneering XK120, offered initially in Open Two Seater form and later supplemented by more sophisticated Fixed Head and Drophead versions, was succeeded by the XK140, in the same three body styles, in 1954. Essentially the same concept, the XK140s were themselves superseded in 1957 by the XK150s.

The appeal of XKs today is probably based on such intangibles as nostalgia and style, but they can be very practical cars. The performance, even by today's standards, is highly respectable. A top speed of 120mph is still very impressive and the acceleration is surprisingly lively. Inevitably cornering power is a little vintage by today's standards, but this is part of an XK's charm. Nevertheless, many a sporty motorist in his modern car has been surprised to find my XK140 still looming large in his rear view mirror after a twisty section of road.

XKs fall between two periods of cars. They came after the pre-war era of relatively straightforward engineering based on separate chassis and bodies of comparatively simple construction, but before the period of monocoque bodies and ever more sophisticated engineering and complexity. Inevitably they borrowed a little from each era. Retaining a separate chassis must have helped the survival rate, and today this helps the task of restoration. Although not stress-bearing like a monocoque, the bodies were of more complex unit design than many pre-war cars and can present difficulties, both in terms of corrosion and rebuilding. The engines have proved their practicality by remaining in volume production for 38 years.

Availability of spare engine parts is excellent, and this obviously assists practicality today. Furthermore, all body panels, items of trim and a number of mechanical parts are being re-manufactured today. Indeed, as time passes it becomes easier to restore and run an XK. As demand increases, so supply obliges.

XKs are increasingly sought today, but it has not always been so. They went through a dark period in the sixties. Each model was inevitably overshadowed by its successor in the fifties, with a consequent diminution of values. But all were dealt a devastating blow by the introduction of the E-type in 1961.

The E-type was as great a step forward as the XK120 had been in 1948 – the E-type made all the XKs seem desperately old-fashioned. The image and value of XKs took a dive. As the sixties progressed, nobody wanted old XKs. Sentiment had not yet entered into the equation, and they were just out-dated models. The older they were, the more out-dated they seemed: the 120s suffered the most and examples could change hands for less than £50.

In the early seventies the trend slowly began to reverse as collecting old cars became fashionable. Modern car design became increasingly dictated by legislation and character was sacrificed – demands of economic mass production had the same effect. Many people felt the need for something more interesting, something that would exude personality and individuality. As the growth of the classic car movement mushroomed through the seventies, so the financial and aesthetic appreciation of XKs was reincarnated.

Paradoxically, the oldest became the most desirable. As the first of the line, the XK120 was to many the purest design and, as a result of its age, perhaps the rarest and most desirable. The 140s and 150s followed the trend but remained poor cousins. Of all the models, the open ones – particularly the roadsters – were the most sought. The XK120 Open Two Seater Super Sports, as it was called at launch, was the original, and the one to have. After rocketing in value, sometimes by more than tenfold, through the seventies, the XK graph seemed to level off and climb more gently through the early eighties. During this time, though, the other XKs caught up and began to be appreciated for their undoubted qualities.

To say that every model of XK is different might seem a simplistic and obvious statement, but it is true in a deeper sense. Appreciation is an emotional matter as well as a subjective one. To some the style of one model appeals most. To others, rarity, extra seats, improved braking or early memories dictate choice. To others again, one model can be a stepping stone to another if price decides choice.

There appear to be three levels of XK in terms of values.

The top group includes all the 120s, the 140 roadsters and Dropheads and the 150 roadsters. The 150 Dropheads occupy the middle ground, although they are said to be even harder to find than 150 roadsters. The poorer cousins are still the 140 and 150 Fixed Head coupés, although some enthusiasts will tell you that they regard the 140 FHC as the classic XK, which just goes to show there is healthy disagreement on the subject. Some people inevitably buy XKs for their investment potential, while others, probably a good majority, purchase an XK knowing that they can indulge themselves in a rewarding hobby without losing money.

With more open cars now being manufactured, it will be interesting to see the effect on the values of older cars. Will demand decrease as people find that there could be a more modern practical alternative, or will the new convertibles introduce a new and wider audience to the pleasures of open air motoring?

One can assume that the rarer and older XKs will appreciate more quickly in the future than the others. I imagine that the XK120 roadster will always be the absolute classic, and will appreciate considerably. The early aluminium-bodied 120 roadsters have a certain cachet, although the steel cars are far better to drive. Gradually people will realise that the XK120 Fixed Head and the XK140 roadster, in genuine right-hand drive form, are extremely rare cars. The XK150 'S' models, especially in roadster guise, are also far from plentiful in right-hand drive form. On the other hand, the practicality of the Drophead models is a distinct merit.

The panel shows the original worldwide distribution of XK models split into export and home deliveries. Particularly in its XK120 days, the model enjoyed cult status in the USA, and the vast majority went to those shores. Many were owned by film stars and other celebrities and a number were raced. Several racing drivers cut their teeth on XKs before moving on to greater heights – Phil Hill, America's first World Champion, is just one example.

In the late eighties, a comparatively large number of XKs have crossed the Atlantic back to Britain and often on to mainland Europe. But a good proportion of the world's XKs do still reside in the USA although the quirks of dollar/sterling/yen/mark/franc relationships mean that examples are continually moving around the globe. Indeed, XKs crop up in the most unlikely places, having been taken there originally or imported over the years. Today, XK enthusiasm is spread widely through many countries, fostered by active clubs. To many owners, originality is very important.

XK120

BODY

In very simple terms, the XK120 Open Two Seater Super Sports bodyshell consisted of front and rear sections joined together by a pair of internal sills, with the doors hung from the front section. This front section was made up of a fabricated sheet steel scuttle in the shape of an inverted 'U'. Incorporated in this was a firewall with door hinge pillars in the 'A' posts. To this scuttle were welded the front wings which provided the largest part of the front bodywork. These front wings were large, complex panels with curves of differing radii. At the front they wrapped around virtually to meet each other, and were joined by a small welded panel below the radiator grille. These welded seams, and the wing-to-bulkhead seams, were leaded over to become invisible.

The steel front wings were made of two main pieces split vertically in the middle of the wheelarch, although one would not be aware of this from the exterior. The headlamp

pod was a separate item, again welded on and leaded. On later cars the same method was used for the sidelight housings. The bonnet was made of aluminium, hinged at the rear and braced at the front, middle and rear. To the front wings were attached inner wings either side of the engine. After November 1951, the front wing sides incorporated a crude fresh air ventilation system operated by opening a small flap to direct air into the footwell area.

The rear body section comprised a folded panel behind the cockpit attached to a pair of inner wings which in turn met the spare wheel floor and cross-bracing to support the wooden boot floor. To the outer edge of the inner wings were welded tonneau panels which ran from the cockpit to the rear. The area between these narrow tonneau panels was covered by a broad, gently curved panel with welded and leaded seams.

Located between the tonneau panels was a bootlid made of aluminium folded over a steel strip and braced by a wooden frame. The rear wings were bolted to the tops of the inner wings where they met the tonneau panels. Beading, or piping, was inserted between the two surfaces. To the front of each rear wing was attached a vertical shut face panel, which was supported internally by a fabricated

pillar closed off from the wheel side by a splash panel. The rear wheelarch was covered by a removable steel spat on cars fitted with pressed steel wheels. On wire wheel cars, the lip on the wing where the spat located was covered by 'D' section brass bead.

Until 14 April 1953, the wing piping was made of rexine (leather cloth) covered cord which matched the body colour. This 4in wide grained material was wrapped over the cord and stitched to leave a tongue to be inserted between the panels. After this date, self-coloured PVC piping was used. This is a good indication of whether a car produced prior to this date is as original as it purports to be.

Front and rear body sections, which could be removed as units, were welded to fabricated steel internal sills. These sills were attached to two body rockers protruding on either side of the main chassis legs. The floors were made of 9mm plywood and screwed to the sills, propshaft cover and transmission cover, which themselves were screwed to each other in the middle and to the front and rear bulkheads.

The doors were made of aluminium and attached by two hinges – there were no check straps. Two six volt batteries were carried behind the seats and enclosed by a lift-off cover.

Early aluminium-bodied cars, although of similar external appearance, were of rather different internal construction. Wood was employed extensively in the traditional coachbuilding way, particularly in the rear section.

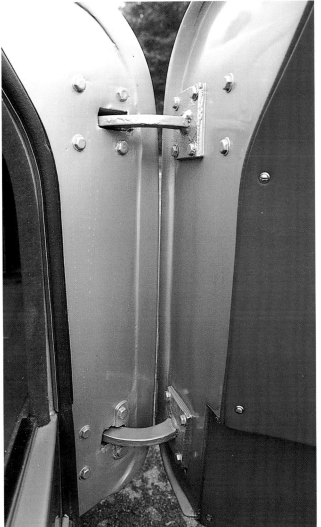

opposite
On wire wheel cars the protruding spinners precluded the fitting of spats, and so 'D' section brass beading was rivetted to the wing flange to improve appearance.

left
Door hinges were regrettably not fitted with any means of lubrication and wear can occur. Replacing the two hinge boxes inside the front wings is quite a major job, although roadsters, with their lighter doors, do not suffer so badly from this problem. Many owners have fitted grease nipples when rebuilding cars to eradicate this problem. Although not original, the modification is unseen and certainly a sensible solution.

above
Part of the appeal of the 120s and 140s surely is the way the wing line drops and rises so dramatically, as shown in this photograph of Alan Minchin's XK140 OTS (which is featured in the next chapter). The wing piping on this car does not match the body colour, which the owner feels is incorrect. With one dissension, our experts agreed.

The XK120 Fixed Head Coupé in right-hand
drive form is a very rare car, as fewer than 200
were produced. Epsom race course makes an
excellent backdrop to Michael and Peter Sargent's
example.

opposite, top
In the style of the day, the rear window was not
exactly generous in size, but it is very adequate
in practice; anything larger would have surely
ruined the balanced shape.

opposite, bottom
The addition of the simple roof merged most
successfully with the original shape, and made a
very different and more sophisticated XK120,
ideal for touring or business.

The XK120 Fixed Head's main structural difference, of course, was the addition of a steel roof as an integral part of the body. Unlike the roadster, its windscreen pillars were of sheet steel. The central rear tonneau panel extended only from the top of the bootlid to the roof, and so was a much smaller panel. An additional panel was used between the upper front edge of the rear wing and below the opening rear quarterlight.

The doors had conventional chrome-plated window frames and wind-up windows with quarterlights and some Fixed Heads had steel doors. The fronts of the doors and the adjoining 'A' post area turned at right angles from the body side line, whereas the roadster's panels were angled with the inner face nearer the rear of the car.

The XK120 Drophead coupé shared the same basic construction as the roadster, but also had the same variations as the Fixed Head (except for the roof). This model therefore had integral windscreen pillars, which continued across the top of the windscreen to form a header panel to which the hood was fixed. It also had the more shallow central tonneau panel, the hood support panel above the front of the rear wings, fixed window frames and the right-angle door hinge faces.

Although the manufacture of some panels was originally subcontracted by Jaguar, all the panels were purchased from the company. No panels are obtainable from Jaguar today and sadly the tooling is long gone. However, the XK restorer need have no fears on this score for there are several specialists in Britain who manufacture all minor panels, front and rear wings, complete front and rear body sections, and even complete bodies.

As for interchangeability, no 150 panels can be used on a 120, and only a few 140 panels can be fitted. The 140's rear wings appear identical but have a cut-out to take a bumper iron. Similarly, 120 and 140 front wings are very similar and vary only at the rear edge – they can usually be adapted. The exception is the 140 FHC as this has a shorter wing. The 120's bootlid will fit no other model. The doors from a 120 DHC are the same as those from a 140 DHC except that the 120 ones have a higher interior cut-out at the bottom as the 120 has a higher sill.

As for interchangeability between different models of 120, the rear wings, bonnets, front and rear splash panels, ventilator box assemblies, front wing valances, spats (in theory), rear number plate plinth, petrol filler box, boot floor and spare wheel tray panels can be used on all three models. All 120 bootlids ought to be interchangeable, but the wooden frame can distort and change the curvature of the panel.

A standard list of body colours (see page 41) was available, although other colours could be supplied to special order. As this applies also to interior trim, there may be occasional exceptions to the general rule.

Specialists generally agree that the engine compartment and underbody areas were finished in black at first and body colour later.

opposite
The XK120 Drophead Coupé, introduced in April 1953, combined the virtues of the Open Two Seater and the Fixed Head, although perhaps it lost a little something in its styling. This car is owned by Dutch Jaguar restorer Pieter Zwakman.

above
With a sophisticated folding hood, the XK120 DHC was undeniably a more practical open XK, appealing to a different clientele.

left
The XK120 DHC was in production for less than 18 months and so rather fewer were made than the roadsters, but the level of sales in that time was very healthy.

BODY TRIM

Part of the XK120's charm is its lack of body trim, which allows the pure, clean shape of the car to be fully appreciated.

At the front the car was fitted with slender, delicate chromed bumpers which were more for appearance than practicality. There appear to be two types of fluting, but in reality the centre ridge probably disappeared as the tooling wore out. It would seem that the bumper irons were usually painted body colour, although black was also used. On top of the bonnet was a badge of copper coloured metal and cream enamel which featured in its centre the Jaguar head. The radiator grille was made up of an approximately oval surround to which 12 vanes were brazed – earlier cars had flutes on the vanes. On top of the headlamp pods were two chromed 'spears'.

The windscreen, with its chrome-plated frame and pillars, was removable on the roadsters, and a small competition-type aeroscreen and cowling could be substituted on one or both sides. A cowl was also available for the rear view mirror. These items were supplied initially with all Special Equipment models, to be used if required, but later were available to special order only. On the aluminium cars both straight and curved side pillars were fitted, but none of these is interchangeable with the steel cars.

At the rear there were no bumpers, just a pair of overriders. These are often mounted upside-down today – they should have the broader side section to the top. The number plate was carried on a separate sheet metal plinth mounted to the lower area of the bootlid, with wing piping between. The bootlid was opened by means of a lockable, chromed 'T' handle situated at the bottom rear of the lid. The fuel filler, a lockable hinged flap, was located on the left-hand tonneau panel, but was situated further to the rear on DHC models. Ace type number plates were fitted and when required later by legislation, small reflectors were added at the bottom corners of the bootlid.

opposite, top left
The distinctive bonnet badge of copper-coloured metal and enamel was one of the first examples of many items now being reproduced for XKs.

opposite, top right
The simple fuel filler lock mechanism was operated by the ignition key and closed onto a rubber seal. The vent pipe seen here is incorrect. There is a breather in the neck and a drain hole in the bottom corner.

opposite, bottom
The delicate grilles were made up of 'bending quality' brass and chrome-plated. Early examples had a raised flute on the front of the vanes and later ones were of a simple 'U' section.

above
The OTS windscreen is made of two pieces of flat glass held in individual 'U' section steel frames which in turn are attached to the cast centre and side pillars.

left
The only rear protection was a pair of overriders, which are often mounted upside down today. This example is correct, but the reflectors, required by law from August 1954, should be fitted (so the factory advised) on the bootlid.

FHC and DHC models had chromed exterior door handles, although they were not interchangeable. All other items of body trim were interchangeable between the 120s, but not with any other models, with the exception of the headlamp spears, the DHC door handles and the OTS 'screen assembly (which fits a 140 OTS). All these items are being remanufactured today, as are all door and boot seals.

FHC and DHC models had additional or alternative items of body trim associated with the windows and roofs. These included side window frames, windscreen chrome trims and a compound curved rear window. None of these items is currently available, but window rubber seals are.

LIGHTS

At a glance, all the headlamps fitted to XK120s appear to be the same, but this is not the case. Most have flat, plain glass lenses and the distinctive tripod arrangement inside, but different lights were fitted for different markets (see list below). Cars for the USA were fitted with more powerful lamps without the tripod arrangement.

Until October 1952, the roadster's front sidelights were placed in small, streamlined, chromed housings fixed to the top of the wing on a rubber gasket. After this date, the housing became an integral part of the wing and was finished in body colour. The sidelight itself increased in diameter at the same time. The smaller sidelights are interchangeable with those of Jaguar Mark II saloons. The large ones are similar in external appearance and size to those used on the 140s and 150s. However, from the same date, these larger sidelights also doubled as flashers on export cars and thus have a double bulb holder to take a twin filament bulb – 140s and 150s had a single filament bulb.

The tail/stop lights were carried in a cast housing. These were chrome-plated on all 120s apart from some cars made during 1951-2, when they were painted body colour. The combined number plate illumination and reverse lamp (Lucas 53159/A – 469) was chrome-plated, including the rear cast body, and its mounting bracket was generally finished in body colour.

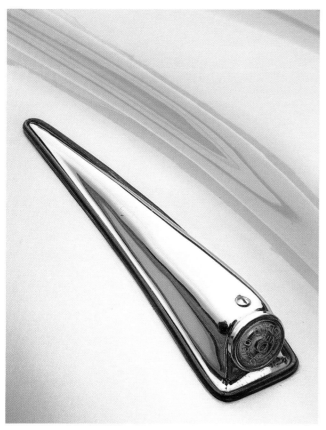

left
Until October 1952, roadsters had separate chrome-plated sidelight housings mounted on a beaded gasket. The light is the same as that on a Mark II saloon, but strictly it should have no lettering on the lens.

top
The number plate was mounted to the body against a rubber seal. The combined reversing/ number plate light should be entirely chrome-plated and fixed to the body colour bracket, as seen here.

opposite, bottom
The chrome-plated windscreen surrounds are another problem area at present, as they are not easily available. It is important that they are not missing when purchasing an XK120 FHC.

opposite, top
Door handles and guttering are examples of items being manufactured today, but FHC window frames are not. Generally these can be rechromed, however, and all the necessary seals are obtainable.

above
The rear lamp housing was cast in 'monkey metal' and, apart from a brief period, chrome-plated. The rubber gasket should have a beaded edge. Lucas still make the lights; they are used on Land Rovers.

All lights are interchangeable between 120 models and all appear to be available today, although that is not true of all the variations of headlamp listed below. Headlamps can be reconditioned on an exchange basis. Remanufactured ones should be carefully examined as some are sub-standard and may even be illegal.

HEADLAMPS

Lucas Part Number	Description
L/H R/H	
all PF. 770	
50838/50839	Home market
50778/A/50779/A	Home market after 660058
50838	R/H drive export
50778/A	R/H drive export after 660058
056244	L/H drive export
50778/A	L/H drive export after 670184
50841/A	Canada & USA
50781/B	Canada & USA afte 660058 670184
50840/A PF.770EF	France only
50780/A PF.770EF	France only after 660058 670184

The chassis consisted of two deep box members running the length of the car. These members diverged as they ran rearwards, and between the cockpit and rear axle they rose up to sweep over the axle. At the top of this 'S' curve the section reduced considerably. These main members were cross-braced at the front ahead of the engine, in the centre by a large box member, and at the rear by a folded sheet steel member and a tube. The fuel tank was suspended on a tray below the high point of the chassis behind the axle.

The body was fixed to the chassis at 12 points as follows: bulkhead, bottom of toe boards to chassis member, two set screws; sills to chassis side brackets, three nuts and bolts plus packing pieces per bracket, two brackets per side; boot area, front to chassis member, two set screws; boot area, rear to chassis member, two nuts and bolts; spare wheel compartment to chassis member, two nuts and bolts. Felt is laid between the body and the chassis. The front inner wing panels were mounted to the chassis at four points on each wing, and each mounting used a nut and bolt.

The chassis was the same for all three 120 models, but differed from later models. The 120 FHC used thicker packing plates at the body mounting points. The chassis should be finished in black, but a high gloss finish is incorrect. New chassis are not available, but they can usually be repaired.

FRONT SUSPENSION

The front suspension was independent, by top and bottom transverse wishbones mounted to a stub axle carrier by upper and lower ball pin assemblies fitted with grease nipples. The wishbones employed Metalastik bushes in their mountings. A Newton telescopic shock absorber connected from the outside point of the lower wishbone to the top of a vertically protruding chassis post.

One type of shock absorber (part number C.3035) was fitted to early chassis numbers as follows: OTS RHD, 660001 to 660679; OTS LHD, 670001 to 672048; FHC RHD, 669001 to 669002; FHC LHD, 679001 to 679621. Subsequent OTS and FHC chassis numbers and all DHC models used another shock absorber, part number C.7183.

Springing was by long 52in splined torsion bars attached at the pivot point of the lower wishbone and to the chassis at the centre box cross member by means of a reaction lever and clamp bolt. Adjustment was possible here with the aid of the barrel nut, trunnion and bolt. An anti-roll bar was fitted and mounted in rubber. Essential measurements are: castor angle, 660001–660125 and 670001–670438 5° positive, subsequent numbers 3° positive; camber angle, 1¾° to 2° positive; swivel inclination, 5°; ground clearance, 7⅛in.

Suspension parts were identical on each model. Items available today include all bushes, lower ball pins and related parts, top ball joints, hub bearings and shock absorbers (Koni & Spax). Suspension parts should be finished dull black.

REAR SUSPENSION

Rear suspension was by silico-manganese steel semi-elliptic leaf springs (with seven leaves) attached at their front within the main chassis member just in front of where it sweeps up. The rear end of each spring was anchored by a shackle which hung from the more slender rear chassis leg. The axle was attached to the springs by two 'U' bolts per side. Two rear axle rebound straps passed under the axle casing and were attached to the chassis. At the strap's lowest point was a rubber buffer to cushion the axle during excessive suspension travel. The springs were covered by leather gaiters. Free camber was 5½in (spring camber is measured from the centres of the spring eyes to the top of the main leaf), and a 585lb load would flatten the spring.

Handed lever-type shock absorbers of Girling (PV.7) manufacture were fitted on the inner sides of the main chassis members and via a link arm to the axle. L/H rear shock absorber C.3753 and R/H rear shock absorber C.3752 were fitted to earlier cars. L/H rear shock absorber C.7214 and R/H rear shock absorber C.7215 were fitted from chassis numbers 660986, 669003, 672280, 679729, 667001 and 677001.

Springs, gaiters and bushes are available today; the shock absorbers can be reconditioned.

REAR AXLE

XKs were fitted with a conventional solid rear axle and differential by means of hypoid crown wheel and pinion attaching to splined half shafts.

Initially, ENV axles were used, but from chassis numbers 660935, 671797, 669003 and 679222 XK 120s were fitted with either ENV or Salisbury back axles. The ENV axle was available with the following ratios: 3.64:1, 3.27:1, 3.92:1, 4.30:1 and 4.56:1. The Salisbury 2HA was available with the following: 3.77:1, 4.09:1 and 4.27:1. From April 1953, Salisbury 4HA axles were fitted and available with the following: 2.93:1, 3.31:1, 3.54:1, 3.77:1, 4.09:1 and 4.27:1.

Apart from the brake back plates, hubs and handbrake cable assembly, the two makes of axle are interchangeable as complete units, but individual parts are not. Bearings and seals are the only parts available today, but Salisbury axles can be reconditioned by GKN. The axle casing was finished in black enamel.

BRAKES

Lockheed hydraulic dual leading shoe 12in drum brakes were used front and rear. A Lockheed master cylinder was mounted to the outer side of the main chassis frame, the side depending on whether the car was right-hand or left-hand drive. A fly-off handbrake was fitted. In April 1952, self-adjusting front brakes and a tandem master cylinder were adopted.

The front brake drums differ on cars fitted with wire wheels and thus are not interchangeable between steel disc and wire wheel cars. Brake linings, hoses, wheel cylinders, master cylinder repair kits and drums for wire wheel cars are available today.

STEERING

The XK120 employed a Burman recirculating ball type steering unit to which was attached a straight column without any universal joint, raked at an angle of 10° to the horizontal. The unit was connected to the nearside stub axle by means of a drop arm, track rod and idler arm. This method of steering was used only on 120s, but is interchangeable between the three body styles. All items should be finished in dull black. Only the track rod ends are obtainable today.

A black Bluemel steering wheel was fitted, although it seems that a few cars, mainly for export, had white examples. The wheel, which is not the same as that on the Mark VII saloon, was adjustable for reach on the column.

WHEELS

Initially 5in wide pressed steel disc wheels were fitted to the 120s, but from May 1952 they were increased in width by ½in. All XK wheels of all models and type were 16in diameter.

Solid steel wheels were fitted with wheel discs, known today as hub caps. To these was affixed a central badge with the word 'Jaguar' on a black background. The sunken areas of the chrome-plated hub caps were finished in body colour. On these cars the rear wing spats were fitted by means of a coach lock and 'T' bar which was inserted through a small escutcheon located at the top centre of the panel and covered

Pressed steel wheels were always finished in body colour and the two sunken areas on the hub caps were given the same finish. This feature is not easy to identify here as the body colour and chrome plate look so similar.

below
Another XK120 OTS, this one owned by Stuart Holden, showing off its wire wheels.

bottom
Many cars have been converted to wire wheels, but the majority left the factory with pressed steel wheels; in this form cars were fitted with rear spats.

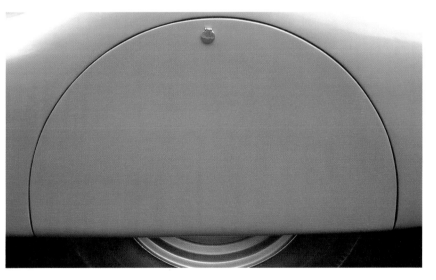

by a hinged flap. The spats located on two small pegs which protruded from the bottom of the wheelarch in front of and behind the wheel.

The wheels were finished in body colour and can be used on any other XK fitted with five stud hubs. Hub caps from a Mark II saloon will fit, but the rim on a 120 is less deep. Pressed steel 15in wheels from other Jaguars cannot be fitted as the pitch is different, nor can 15in hubs be fitted to XK rear axles as the taper on the halfshaft differs.

Special Equipment models were fitted with 54-spoke wire wheels, which were also an option on the standard cars. The wheels can be interchanged with all XKs fitted with splined hubs. Smaller 15in wheels from the Mark II saloons can be fitted but are not correct. Wire wheels were available in body colour, silver and chrome-plated. Part-chromed wire wheels were also available with varnished rims finished in Dunlop Wheel Silver. They are retained by two-eared, chrome-plated and sided spinners or knock-off nuts. These fit all models of XK with wire wheels. Chrome wire wheels, spinners and splined hubs are available today.

TYRES

From the factory 120s were fitted with Dunlop Roadspeed 6.00 x 16 tyres, although Dunlop racing tyres of the same size could be supplied to special order. An inner tube was, of course, fitted.

Tyres of this size have been difficult to obtain in recent years, but Dunlop RS5s and Avon Turbospeeds are once more available. Today some people prefer to fit radial tyres, and Pirelli Cinturatos can usually be obtained (at a price).

Period photographs show some cars, mainly those in the USA, with whitewall tyres. It is believed that few, if any, 120s left the factory with these.

INTERIOR TRIM

XKs were fitted with two seats with lift-out cushions and hinged squabs which met in the middle, like a bench seat. They were covered in leather with moquette on the back of the squabs. They were adjustable and mounted on frames which were either a grey/green colour or chrome-plated. The seats give the appearance of being similar between models, but the backs were in fact different. OTS seats had a cut-out near the outside on their backs to clear the stowed hood, FHC seats had no cut-outs and DHC seats had very slim backs. The sculpting on the squabs seems to have varied with some being virtually straight across the car and others having more individual shape. Between the cushions was a fluted, padded cover over the propshaft tunnel.

The seats could be ordered in two-tone trim, in which case the 11 fluted panels on 120 roadsters were covered in the lighter colour, and the outer panels and piping in a darker colour matching the rest of the trim. The most common two-tone colour scheme was red and beige. Connolly hide was employed whenever leather was used in XKs, but as the

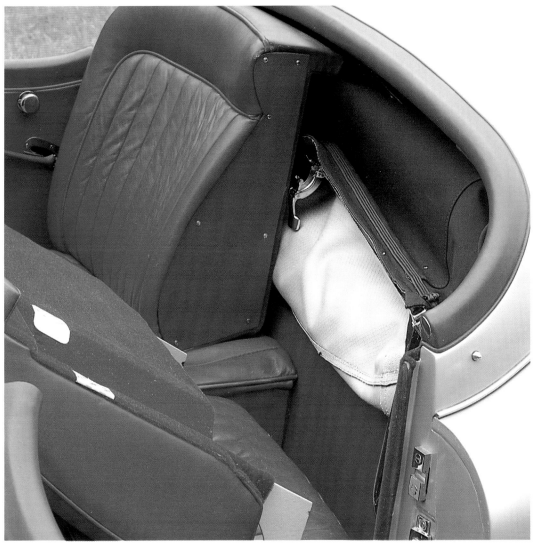

opposite
Even the more stark OTS interior was luxurious by sports car standards of the period. The seats are comfortable, but do not give much lateral location.

left
The rather crude roadster hood stowed very neatly behind the seats and necessitated cut-outs on the seat backs to clear the hood frame. The side screens were stowed under the panel finished with the leather-covered cockpit roll.

below left
The fly-off handbrake works as a splendid anti-theft device today as few people understand how to work one, merely pulling it on harder and harder! Gear knobs are available today.

below
The wooden floor was carpeted, as was the transmission tunnel. The dipswitch (visible top left of the clutch pedal) should have a rubber cap and the bonnet pull (top left) was generally a knurled chromed knob.

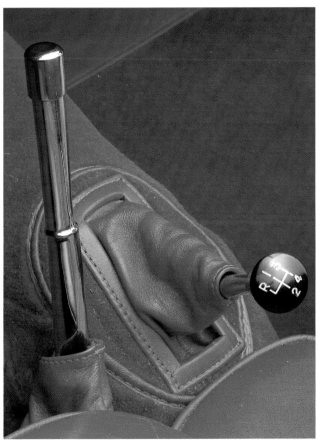

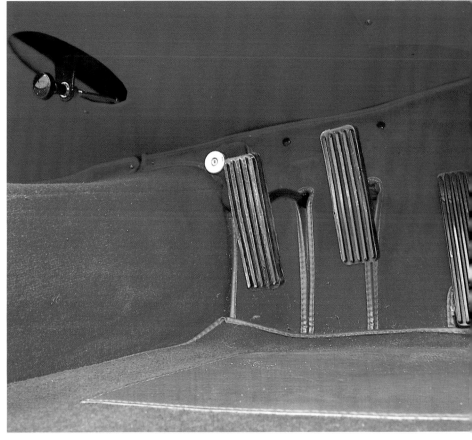

process has changed over the years it is no longer possible always to obtain the exact colour.

A cockpit roll of rubber covered in leather with chrome 'bungs' in the ends was fitted to the scuttle, doors and tonneau panel. The lengths, respectively, were 43½in, 27½in (x 2) and 64½in. The floor and transmission tunnel were covered with carpet, its edges bound with rexine. There was a correct number of stitches per inch, but this is a trade secret! The driver's side carpet had a 15in x 8½in PVC-coated felt heel pad stitched to it. In some instances this stitching formed a cross, although I am told that this pattern does not wear well and soon breaks away.

Rexine-covered panels were used to the sides and tops of the footwells with an opening to be able to operate the vent boxes and to allow the ingress of air on cars so fitted. The gear lever was surrounded by a gauntlet made from leather and clasped by a 'Standard Insulator Type C' hose clip. The

handbrake had a similar hide gaiter. The firewall-mounted dipswitch was surrounded by a small piece of moquette and covered by a rubber cap, and the bonnet pull was a chromed, knurled metal knob situated above the knees. Pedals were covered in ribbed rubbers.

Door trims were covered in hide, and incorporated a large silk flocked pocket with a covered black celluloid flap and Tenax fastener. The assembly piping was covered in rexine and the door was opened by the use of a 'pull cord'. The door could be locked internally and the small chrome disc used for this purpose is identical to those used on the much later 420 saloon. On the roadster, two chromed knurled knobs screwed into the door and clasped the side screens when fitted. These side screens, or curtains as they used to be called, were made on a thin metal frame and consisted of a thin sheet of clear perspex set in a chrome-plated brass frame. Below this was an area covered in mohair, incorporating a

covered black celluloid flap which could be hinged upwards to enable one to make hand signals.

The area behind the seats was mostly covered in rexine. A box cover, trimmed in the same material, covered the two batteries.

The roadster's mohair hood had a small perspex window encased in a metal frame with a chrome trim surrounding it. From January 1953, a panel incorporating this rear window could be unzipped on three sides and folded down into the car. A mohair tonneau cover was also supplied which, like the hood, clipped on to the two chrome 'tear drops' on the tonneau panel. At the front it clipped on to the windscreen pillars and the scuttle top. From 1952 this scuttle top was fitted with chromed demister vents.

Later hoods were a little longer, and later side screens had a larger window. These side curtains were stored in a Hardura-covered tray behind the seats and under the tonneau panel. The boot floor was covered in bound carpet, the inner wings were bare and moquette was glued to the petrol filler pipe cover. The underside of the bootlid was fitted with 'KB' quality millboard which was covered in Rexine and incorporated a small interior light mounted in an ash casing.

opposite
All roadster door trim items are available today, as are the seals which run along the sill side, and the seal and chrome bead which runs along the sill top/carpet edge.

above
As wire wheels were slightly larger in width due to the hub protruding outside the rim line, boot panels were slightly revised for these cars. In theory, it is possible to tell whether the car left the factory with wires or not. The boot hinges should be body colour.

right
The 'T' handle for releasing the spats is attached to the petrol filler pipe cover by two chrome-plated Terry's 80/00 spring clips; it should be plain silver. The sides of the boot should not be covered, and the inner wings should be visible, painted body colour.

far right
XKs were jacked up by placing the red jack through a hole in the floors, just ahead of the seats and covered by a plate, and locating the jack into the side of the chassis mounting bracket. This location is plugged by a rubber bung.

bottom
The leather tool roll should carry a valve extractor, adjustable spanner, pliers, tyre lever, distributor screwdriver, feeler gauge, box spanner (torsion bar), three other box spanners, box spanner (sparking plug), short tommy bar, long tommy bar, five open ended spanners, screwdriver, bleeder wrench, tube and container.

above
Like the cockpit floors, the boot floor was made of plywood screwed down with oval shaped washers. All Special Equipment roadsters had a twin exhaust system with a single silencer and chromed ends to the pipes.

top
One of the more unusual optional extras must be the two items of fitted luggage available for XK120s.

right
As the boot area is not exactly square, the fitted suitcases must have proved extremely useful. XK boots, however, are a reasonable size, and it is possible with ingenuity to pack in a good amount of luggage.

left
This roadster interior has a number of later features, including demister vents and indicators. It is also fitted with a period radio slung below the centre dashboard panel.

below
The FHC interior was altogether more luxurious. The seat squabs on these cars had rather more shape than those of the open cars.

bottom
What we call quarterlights were described by Jaguar as 'no draught ventilators'. The simple door trim and map pocket were topped off with the traditional veneered cappings. Note that the bottom panel of the door, which is trimmed on the OTS, is merely painted on the coupés.

The bootlid stay could be finished either in body colour or chrome, while the hinges were body colour.

All these items are available today, or can be made up by a specialist trimmer. The one exception is the unobtainable chrome bead along the front of the hood. Roadster interior mirrors are also obtainable but are longer than those fitted to DHC and FHC models.

The Fixed Head varied in having a walnut dash and door-cappings. It also had an interior door handle and window winder. Across the lower section of the door trim was a shallow pocket suitable for slim maps. The headlining was made of wool, in fawn or grey, but there were no sun visors. In the rear quarters were located two interior lights operated by a switch on the dash. Behind the seats a flap lifted to reveal a storage compartment, which in turn tilted forward to reveal the two six volt batteries. The dash top and a collar on the steering column were trimmed in rexine to match the seats, which on this model had 10 flutes.

Interior door handles are interchangeable between FHC and DHC models and available today, as are the chrome-plated finger pulls which are fixed to the top of the door trims

top left
The window catches on the FHC rear quarterlights are similar – but not identical – to those used on other Jaguars, such as Mark II saloons. Those on the XK120 should be plain, without hatching in the 'thumb' area. The interior lights are not yet being remanufactured.

far left
The area behind the seats has a lid which folds back to reveal a useful stowage area. The box is trimmed in headlining material. Trimming experts say that the hinges should be concealed by overlapping rexine.

left
The stowage box tilts forward to reveal two six volt batteries. Unfortunately it is not possible to obtain the correct period-looking batteries today.

on both Fixed Head and Drophead models.

The Drophead interior was very similar in style to that of the Fixed Head. The flat surface behind the seats was fitted with rubber rubbing strips. On this model, the seats had just nine flutes.

The DHC's mohair hood was a much more elaborate affair than the roadster's. Apart from being a conventional folding convertible type, it had an inner headlining which made the mechanism invisible. With the aid of two zips, the solid rear window unzipped in the same manner as the OTS, but these parts are not interchangeable. The chrome trim surrounding this window is available, and the bead surrounding the hood base can be made. This is not a half-round section, as often believed, but a 'P' section, for the hood envelope clips over this. Similarly, the chrome bead on the hood above the window can be specially made but is expensive. The hood was clasped to the top rail above the windscreen by three chrome over-centre clips, which are available.

The DHC was as sumptuous as the FHC. When raised, its lined hood gave the impression that you were in a closed car.

31

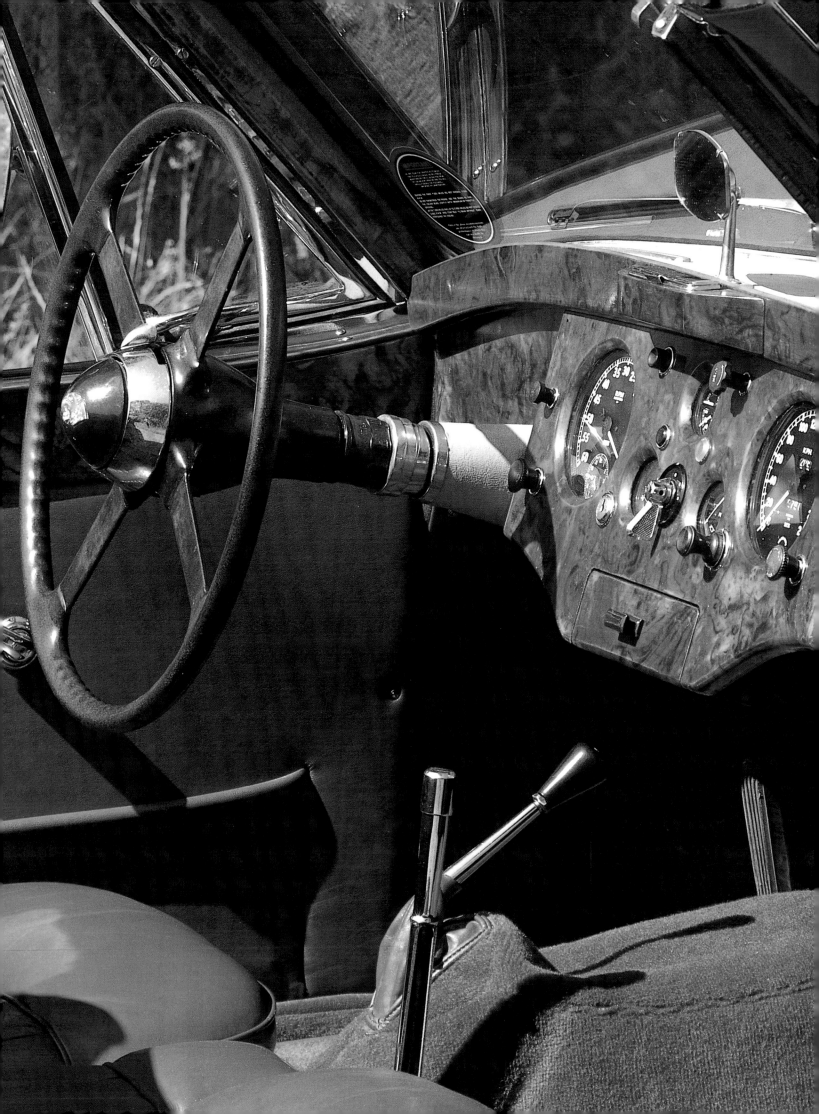

left
It would appear that the trim colour of this car has been changed, for the seats do not match the dash top area and the steering column cover.

This car is fitted with the optional 'cranked' gear lever and, since it is a left-hand drive car, the fly-off handbrake is on the right-hand side of the transmission tunnel.

The rear window could be unzipped to obtain extra ventilation without lowering the hood. The chrome bead around the solid window is available, and is not interchangeable with that of the OTS. The other beads, including the 'P' section one around the base, are not being manufactured.

As the hood mechanism did not fold down behind the seats on DHC models, the rear of the seat squabs did not have such a pronounced cut-out as the OTS model. The batteries were positioned as on the FHC, although on this example there should be rubbing strips on the top area behind the seats.

DASHBOARD AND INSTRUMENTS

The OTS dash was covered in leather to match the seats and the centre section was angled outwards at the bottom. When two-tone seats were fitted, the main face of the dash matched the lighter, inner, fluted panels of the seats, and the piping around the base matched the outer panels of the seats, door trims and carpet. A chrome-plated grab handle was fitted in front of the passenger. If an optional radio was fitted, it was hung below the central panel.

The major instruments were a Smiths speedometer and tachometer (incorporating clock), and the minor ones were a combined Smiths fuel gauge and oil level gauge (operated by a Lucas black push button on the dash, deleted on later cars), combined Smiths water temperature and oil pressure gauge and Lucas ammeter. The cigar lighter was made by Smiths but the light switch, starter button, ignition switch, ignition warning light, panel light switch, and windscreen wiper switch were Lucas parts. The cigar lighter on earlier cars had a glass centre.

Later cars, after September 1952, had a different dash layout and included a heater control switch and flasher warning light. On earlier cars the ignition switch was placed at the top to the right of the tachometer, but on later cars it moved to a lower position to the bottom right of the same instrument.

The instruments are interchangeable between XK120 models, but remember that the speedometers differed depending on back axle ratio. Although the instruments are not available today, they can usually be rebuilt, and, in the case of the speedometers, recalibrated as required.

The Fixed Head dash was of entirely different construction, material and appearance to that of the OTS, but the layout and make of instruments and switches was similar. The dash was a wooden one with walnut veneer. In front of the passenger was a glove box with lockable lid. A single chrome-plated ashtray was mounted at the centre top of the dash and at centre bottom was a small drawer. Both the drawer and the glove box interiors were covered in green flock. There was a push/pull switch for the interior light.

The DHC dash was very similar to that of the FHC.

top
The OTS dashboard was made of steel and covered in leather. On the far right (concealed by the steering wheel) was a black button which, when depressed, converted the petrol gauge into an oil level gauge.

second from top
The car shown here is a later example than the one with the red interior, and thus has a later dashboard with the ignition switch in a lower position.

left
The FHC dashboard was rather more opulent and followed the tradition of the Jaguar saloons in having a walnut veneered facia, although the instrument layout remained similar to the OTS.

above
The DHC dashboard design closely followed that of the FHC. As it did not have an interior light, the switch for that function was deleted.

ENGINE

The six cylinder XK engine had a bore and stroke of 83mm by 106mm which gave a displacement of 3442cc. Compression ratios of either 7:1, 8:1 or 9:1 could be ordered and were denoted by a suffix to the engine number (for example, W.1002/8). The block, made from cast iron, was finished in black, and the sump, an aluminium die casting, was left unpainted. On top of the block was the aluminium alloy cylinder head which on all 120s, including Special Equipment models, was silver in colour. The firing order was 1, 5, 3, 6, 2, 4, with 1 at the rear of the engine.

The inlet manifold, with integral water rail, camshaft covers and oil breather outlet, was also aluminium alloy. Together with the front of the cylinder head, these were polished, but not highly polished as some 'over-bulled' cars are today. Later cars had additional studs at the front of the cam covers (believed to be after November 1951) to remedy oil seepage. Some earlier cars were fitted with a small bar screwed to the head and with lugs resting on the cam covers in an attempt to solve this problem. The camshafts were driven by a two-stage duplex roller chain and the 2¾in diameter EN.16 manganese molybdenum steel crankshaft was carried in seven large Vandervell steel-backed white metal type bearing shells. Connecting rods of EN.16 and Aerolite aluminium alloy solid skirt pistons (with two compression rings and one slotted scraper ring) were used.

It is believed that the plug leads on early cars went round the back of the engine and were located in a gaiter attached to the left-hand head studs. On later cars, the leads took a path over the front right-hand side of the engine and were located by a rubber grommet in a chromed ring, and the gaiter was attached to the right-hand side of the engine 'V' (the left-hand side if viewing the engine from the front).

The standard engine produced 160bhp and the Special Equipment engine (with high lift camshafts) 180bhp. The C-type head, with 1 ⅝in exhaust valves (as opposed to 1 7/16in), later became available to raise output to 210bhp. When fitted to the 120 this was painted silver, the same as the standard heads, and was identifiable by a 'C' cast in the centre.

CARBURETTORS

Three types of twin 1¾in SU H6 carburettors were fitted at different times. Two of the types are externally identifiable: earlier ones have taller tops to the dash pots, and later ones shorter, stubby tops. An auxiliary electric starting carburettor was fitted. On early cars the starting carburettor was integral with the float chamber of the rear carburettor. On later cars it was a separate unit attached to the front carburettor. Fuel was supplied by an SU electric petrol pump, and copper piping was used.

OTS models were fitted with two pancake type air cleaners with black bodies. The other two models had a large drum connected to the carburettors by rubber hoses. A large cylindrical air cleaner was situated at the front of the engine and connected to the 'drum' by a length of flexible tube.

Special Equipment models, with the C-type head, were fitted with larger 2in carburettors easily identifiable by the 'rough cast' squarer-bodied dash pots.

Most parts are available for rebuilding the SU carburettors, and there are firms who specialise in this.

COOLING SYSTEM

Coolant circulated from the lower region of the radiator, mounted upright on the 120, by way of the water pump through the water passages in the block, the cylinder head and the inlet manifold water rail, before returning to the radiator header tank. A thermostat situated in the water rail outlet elbow recirculated water until sufficient temperature had been reached, when it allowed full circulation through the radiator. The system was pressurised and usually fitted with a 4lb circular cap, without ears. An overflow pipe ran from the filler neck down the side of the radiator.

The polished cast aluminium fan, fitted on earlier cars and mounted on the water pump spindle, was driven by a 'V' belt from the crankshaft pulley. Later cars had a fabricated steel fan. The radiator, which should be a dull black, has a brass drain tap positioned on the front at the bottom, and there is a chromed engine drain tap sited at the nearside rear of the block.

Radiators can be re-cored and water pumps rebuilt. Reproduction pumps and all hoses (attached with Jubilee clips) are also available. The parts are interchangeable between models of 120 but not with other XKs.

EXHAUST

All models were fitted with two cast iron three-into-one exhaust manifolds. These should be vitreous enamelled, although this finish does not last if the car is used. Standard cars were fitted with a single system and thus the downpipe went from two into one as it curved to run rearward through the chassis central crossmember. It had a short flexible section before joining the single silencer. Four different tail pipes were fitted at different times and it seems that certainly some, if not all, emerged under the nearside rear wing behind the wheel. The end of the pipe was polished or chrome-plated.

Special Equipment models were fitted with what was termed a twin pipe racing type exhaust. Two pipes ran from the manifolds under the chassis central box member to a single silencer and emerged at the rear of the car. From March 1953, SE FHCs reverted to a single system.

Exhaust systems are interchangeable between 120s and are being re-manufactured today. Stainless steel is obviously not original but highly practical.

ELECTRICS

A Lucas dynamo was used, the exact model depending on the compression ratio of the engine. A 45012/A-B. 12/L coil, 76411/D-ST.950 starter solenoid, either 26042/E-M.45G/GC.47 or 26062/A-M.45G/GC.47 starter, 37076/D-RF. 95/2-L.4 control box and 37110/A-SF.4/L.23 fuse box, complete with cover, were fitted from the same source.

As for sparking plugs, 7:1 compression ratio engines were fitted with Champion L.10S plugs, 8:1 with L.11S, and 9:1 with NA.12. Engines being used for racing purposes used L.11S if 7:1 and NA.10 if 8:1.

A Lucas 69032-WT.29U 'low-note' horn and 69033-WT.29U 'high-note' horn should be fitted, with relay box 33116/A-SB.40/L.2 for earlier cars (up to and including 660784 and 671097) and 33135/B-SB.40/1 on later cars.

The torpedo-type horn push was the same as used on the Mark V saloon but fitted upside-down and without the indicator switch, unless indicators were fitted. Late cars, from September 1954, had a flat horn push, as fitted to the 140s, in place of the torpedo-type.

OTS models were fitted with three different types of Lucas wiper motor, and FHC models used a fourth type.

The main wiring consisted of separate harnesses for the body, instrument panel, engine (which used a Lucas junction box), chassis, boot and (for export models) flasher units. There were earth leads from the engine to the chassis, from the body to the engine, for the petrol pump, sidelamps and (on FHC models) interior lights.

Newly made harnesses, including original-type cloth-covered items, can be obtained today, and most electrical parts can be reconditioned.

TRANSMISSION

The clutch, a single plate Borg & Beck unit with a 10in diameter plate, was enclosed in an aluminium alloy bell housing. The Moss-type gearbox had four forward gears and reverse; first and reverse were without synchromesh. The main casing was cast iron, and a separate light alloy casing enclosed the rear of the mainshaft. The main casing was finished in black, while the bell housing, gearbox top and rear casing were silver. The gear ratios were 3.375:1 first, 1.982:1 second, 1.367:1 third and direct top.

Jan 1950

Engine oil capacity increased to 29 Imp pints (28.8 US pints/13.6 litres), dipstick maximum mark altered to 8 1/16in (205mm) below the collar.

Timing gauge included in toolkit

Steering track rod bearings: thread bearing replaced by rubber bearings requiring no lubrication. Track rod end grease nipples deleted.

Apr 1950

Blanking plates supplied with cars for fitting to brake air scoops, if desired, to prevent dirt or water entering brakes.

Jul 1950

New Ferobestos socket adopted for lower wishbone assembly to eradicate low speed steering wobble. Greaser replaced by plug.

Aug 1950

From: OTS 660126/670439
Castor angle changed from 5° positive to 3° positive.

Fitment of individual air cleaners standardised (does not apply to later FHC and DHC models).

Dec 1950

Newton front shock absorbers – filler plug deleted.

Jan 1951

Mintex M.15 brake linings superseded by M.14.

Mar 1951

Modifications introduced to ENV axles affecting interchangeability.

Nov 1951

From: Engine No. W.3686
Boss for fitting engine heater element incorporated in block at the rear left side, above and slightly forward of the dipstick.

From: OTS 660675/671097
Footwell ventilators fitted in front wings.

Alterations adopted on connecting rods, still interchangeable in sets.

From: OTS 660911/671493
'Air conditioner unit' without demisting or defrosting to the windscreen fitted as standard.

From: Engine No. W.3593 to W.3596 inclusive, and from W.3635
Mark VII saloon type stepped sump adopted. Capacity now 24 Imp pints (28 US pints/13.5 litres).

Feb 1952

From: Engine No. W.4052
Altered timing chain tensioner adopted.

From: OTS 660935/671797
FHC 669003/679222
Salisbury axles with 3.77:1 ratio fitted to some cars.

From: OTS 660935/671797
FHC 669003/679215
Short main shaft gearbox without rear extension adopted, plus longer propshaft and different length speedo cable.

Apr 1952

From: Engine No. W.4483
Valve guides altered to fit ⅜in lift camshaft without modification.

Long main shaft gearbox (prefix SH or JH) re-adopted on some cars.

From: Engine No. W.4383
Mark VII type oil filter adopted.

From: OTS 660980/672049
FHC 669003/679622
Self-adjusting front brakes, tandem-type master cylinder fed by a divided supply fluid tank and altered rear brake adjuster adopted.

May 1952

From: Engine No. W.5465
Six-bladed fan and integral pulley and hub adopted.

Jun 1952

From: OTS 660980/672049
FHC 669003/679622
Newton telescopic front shock absorbers (C.7183) with altered valve settings adopted. Diameter now 2⅛in as opposed to 2¾in.

From: OTS 660986/672280
FHC 669003/679729
Girling rear shock absorbers (C.7214 RH, C.7215 LH) with altered valve settings adopted. Girling part number (71 RH, 72 LH) stamped on top.

Oct 1952

From: Engine No. W.6149
Oil level indicator and element no longer fitted to sump. Blanking plate fitted instead.

From: Gearbox No. JL.13154
Altered top cover and reverse striking rod adopted.

Alteration made to auxiliary starting carburettor switch-plunger (identifiable by green spot on front cover).

From: OTS 661025/672963

Front wings altered to have integral sidelight housing (body colour). Export cars wired so that light unit doubled as indicator. Relay fitted.

From: OTS 661025/672963

Demister vents for windscreen adopted and connected to heater unit by flexible hoses, as on FHC.

Conversion available to convert British-type headlamps to US-type sealed beam units.

Dec 1952

From: Gearbox Nos. JL.13834/SL.6313A
Synchronising sleeve on first and second gears fitted with stop pin.

From: OTS 661040/673320
     FHC 669003/679222
Rear springs, as fitted to SE models, adopted. This spring has five 7/32in leaves and two 3/16in leaves as against three 7/32in leaves and four 3/16in leaves of previous type.

From: OTS Body No. F.5272, and certain nos. 5082 to 5272
FHC Body No. J.2375, and certain nos. 2223 to 2368
Cars sprayed with synthetic enamel paint
One pint tin of Quick Drying Enamel supplied with each car despatched overseas. Packed in fibre-board carton and located under spare wheel.

From: OTS 661037/673009 + 661026, 661028, 661029
     FHC 669003/680271 + 680167, 680168, 680169
Trico vacuum-operated windscreen washer fitted, consisting of a glass water container mounted on the engine side of the scuttle, connected to jets at the base of the windscreen. Water delivered to the jets by a vacuum-operated pump incorporated in the water container cap. The top pipe of the pump connected to the inlet manifold via a chrome-plated control on the instrument panel.

From: OTS 661042/673298
     FHC 669003/680477
Pressed steel wheel rim width increased to 5½in.

FHC models now provided with two keys: one for ignition, doors and petrol filler locks; one for boot lid and cubby box locks.

From: OTS 661046/673396
Modified type of hood rear panel adopted. Opened by unzipping both sides in an upward direction, unzipping the base of the panel and disconnecting the fastener. The panel retained in the open position by raising the bottom edge and attaching the fasteners to the studs provided on one of the hood sticks.

Removable plate adopted on right side of transmission tunnel for access to UJ and grease nipples.

Feb 1953

FHC models with remote air cleaner situated behind radiator, weaker WO 2 needles adopted in place of RF carburettor needles.

Mar 1953

From: FHC 669005/680738
SE cars fitted with single exhaust, as opposed to twin previously fitted. OTS SE still twin.

From: Engine No. W.7207
Altered water pump adopted.

Apr 1953

From: OTS 661054/673693
     FHC 669007/680880
     DHC 667002/677016
4HA Salisbury axle (3.54) replaced 2HA (3.77)

May 1953

From: Engine No. W.8275
Lightened flywheel, as fitted to SE models, adopted on all models.

From: Engine No. W.8381
Malleable iron crankshaft torsional vibration damper superseded cast iron item.

June 1953

From: Engine No. W.8643
Altered con rods with increased length cap bolt bosses adopted.

From: OTS 661078/674006
     FHC 669021/681203
     DHC 667002/677286
Altered speedometer cable adopted.

From: OTS 661075/673995
     FHC 669021/681200
     DHC 667002/677242
Altered rev counter cable adopted.

Aug 1953

All Home Market and Home Leave cars fitted with ignition suppressors.

Sep 1953

OTS SE models: racing screens and cowls previously supplied, now to special order only.

From: Gearbox No. JL.18457
Strengthened speed forks adopted.

Jan 1954

Altered tappet settings adopted for all models (.004in inlet, .006in exhaust; competition setting .006in inlet, .010in exhaust).

From: Gearbox No. SL.9984A
Strengthened speed forks adopted.

JH and JL gearboxes
When fitted with close ratio gears, suffix 'CR' added.

From: OTS 661151/674415
     FHC 669106/681271
     DHC 667161/678085
Modified cigar lighter adopted. 'Mark II' holder has four indents on chrome-plated shoulder, and element has copper-plated ejection spring. Not interchangeable.

Apr 1954

From: Engine No. F.2726
Clutch driven plate C.8401 fitted.

From: Engine No. F.2365
Altered inlet valves with depression in head adopted.

From: Engine No. F.2421
Altered exhaust valves, with reduced stem diameter under head, and shorter, non-counterbored guides adopted.

May 1954

From: Engine No. F.2773
Altered, hard-chromed and polished timing chain tensioner adopted.

Aug 1954

Home Market only.
Two rear reflectors now required on all cars by law. Reflectors (Lucas RER5) to be mounted on bootlid 3¼in from the bottom of the lid and 1⅜in in from the side edges.

Sep 1954

From: OTS 661165 (not 6, 7, 8, 9)/674929 (not 675031–675607)
FHC 669158/681466
DHC 667243/678305
Altered rev counter cable with black polythene outer covering adopted.

From: OTS 661170/675763
FHC 669185/681477
DHC 667271/678390
Altered handbrake adopted.

From: OTS 661172/675926
FHC 669164/681481
DHC 667280/678418
Altered steering column with flat horn push adopted.

SPECIAL EQUIPMENT SPECIFICATION

Special Camshafts with ⅜in lift
Special Crankcraft Damper
Wire Spoke Wheels with Splined Hubs and Knock-On Hub Caps
Dual Exhaust System (on OTS only)
Stiffer Torsion Bars of 1in diameter
Lightened Flywheel
Stiffer Rear Road Springs
Pair of Lucas Fog Lamps.

OPTIONAL EXTRAS

"Note – the following items are supplied to special order only."

Fog Lamp (Lucas 053135/A – SFT.700/S). One or two as required.

Suit Cases (two per set shaped to fit luggage compartment of Open Two-Seater, Fixed Head or Drophead Coupé).

Luggage Rack Assembly.

Car Radio Assembly (Radiomobile RM.100 – consisting of receiver unit, power unit, aerial, etc.)

Following Radiomobile radios also available – 4012, 4014, 4050, RM.4200, RM.4203, RM.4300.

Radio Installation (details required for fitting radio assembly) – various according to radio type.

Auxiliary Petrol Tank.

Hose, connecting auxiliary and main petrol tanks.

Straps securing auxiliary petrol tank.

Main Petrol Tank.

Spare Wheel Mounting when auxiliary petrol tank is fitted.

Racing Screen Assembly, LH & RH (fitted to Special Equipment models, cars bearing chassis number prefix 'S').

Shield Assembly for underside of chassis frame.

Bucket Seat Assembly (racing type).

Floorboard Assembly, LH & RH (for use only when special bucket seats are fitted).

Modified Cylinder Head (C-type), having larger valves and valve throats and modified porting. Available with 2in carburettors.

Special Racing Clutch.

Close Ratio Gearbox.

Alternative axles were available, giving the following ratios: 3.31, 4.09, 4.27, 4.55.

Heater.

Sump Guard.

COACHWORK	INTERIOR OTS	FHC	DHC	HOOD OTS ★	DHC
Suede Green	Suede Green	Suede Green	Suede Green	—	French Grey Black
Ivory		Red Pale Blue	Red Pale Blue	—	Dark Sand French Grey Black
Birch Grey	Red Biscuit	Red Grey Pale Blue	Red Grey Pale Blue	—	French Grey Black
Battleship Grey	—	Red Grey Biscuit	Red Grey	—	French Grey Gunmetal Black
Lavender Grey	—	Red Suede Green Pale Blue	Red Suede Green Pale Blue	—	French Grey Black
Gunmetal	—	Red Grey Pale Blue	Red Grey Pale Blue	—	French Grey Gunmetal Black
Black	Biscuit Pigskin	Tan Red Grey Pigskin Biscuit	Tan Red Grey Pigskin Biscuit	—	Dark Sand French Grey Black Gunmetal
Pale Green Metallic	—	Suede Green Pale Blue Grey	Grey Pale Blue	—	French Grey Black
Dove Grey	—	Tan Biscuit	Tan Biscuit	—	Dark Sand Black
Bronze	Biscuit Tan	—	—	—	—

CHASSIS NUMBERS/DATES

Model	Years Manufactured	Chassis Numbers RHD	LHD
Open Two-Seater (OTS)	1949-1954 ★	660001	670001
Fixed Head Coupé (FHC)	1951-1954	669001	679001
Drophead Coupé (DHC)	1953-1954	667001	677001

★ announced in late 1948, also known as a 'roadster'.

'S' prefix to chassis number indicates Special Equipment model.

Engine Numbers commence: W.1001, followed by F.1001 (Nov '53).
/7, /8 or /9 suffix indicates compression ratio.

In USA: XK120 SE known *unofficially* as XK120M.

XK140

BODY

The XK140's construction was essentially the same as that of its predecessors. Indeed, the car was known at the factory during its gestation period as the XK120 Mark 4. However, there were some significant changes and the three different styles of 140 varied to a greater degree than did the 120s. As the engine was moved forward by 3in, the scuttle could be moved forward a similar amount to improve interior space. The bodyshells remained a mixture of steel and aluminium

panels, although from October 1956 the DHC and FHC models had steel-skinned doors with wooden frames.

The most major changes on the XK140s were made to the rear body section. The boot lid no longer ran to the bottom edge of the body but stopped approximately 6in short. A fixed panel ran from the side tonneau panels to close off this area. By doing this, a well was created in which the spare wheel was positioned. It was hidden from view when the bootlid was opened by a hinged plywood panel, which comprised the major part of the revised boot floor. The front of the spare wheel well had a curved extension piece which was bolted in. This was painted black, but the rest of the area

42

opposite
The XK concept was taken a step further when the evolutionary XK140 was introduced in Drophead Coupé (seen here), Fixed Head Coupé and Open Two Seater forms in October 1954.

above
Cars fitted with pressed steel wheels were still equipped with rear wing spats, and the folded hood was covered by a neat hood bag, as on the 120 DHC.

top
The XK140 retained the classic shape and became a more refined car, but for some the more obtrusive chrome was a retrograde step. This DHC is owned by Barrie Williams.

left
Reservations about the slight dilution of the appearance are today tempered by the fact that many prefer the 140 to drive, although another school of thought feels that the 140 'went soft'.

above
The XK140 Fixed Head Coupé took sophistication a stage further by having a considerably enlarged cabin, with increased legroom and more creature comforts. This car belongs to John Ruff.

left
The XK140 FHC had a longer roof line than its predecessor to give improved headroom, and its larger window assisted rearward visibility.

opposite
The Open Two Seater completed the XK140 trio and, apart from extra chrome, was unchanged in appearance. It benefitted from rack and pinion steering and telescopic rear shock absorbers, and the engine was moved forward by 3in. Alan Minchin owns this car.

was body colour, apart from the black fabricated spare wheel mounting. Specialists are uncertain whether the bootlid stay was body colour or grey.

The XK140's bootlid catch was no longer operated by a sliding rod, which on the 120s located into a small socket on the underside of the tonneau panel. Instead, a system of wires operated two small 'star' wheels which hooked onto two inverted 'U' bolts at the extreme rear corners of the boot floor. The number plate plinth was mounted on the new additional rear panel below the bootlid – PVC piping in body colour was used around this.

On the DHC there were no longer trays in the rear bulkhead for the batteries, but instead a single 12 volt battery was located in the nearside front wing behind the wheel. Here a 'battery box' was positioned and had a door to enable fitting and removal of the battery through the front of the box. The door was retained in position by two Zeus fasteners with butterfly heads. Small horizontal valance panels were fixed to the front of the front wings either side of the grille, and body colour PVC wing piping filled the gap between them.

The rear bulkhead was altered to allow for the provision of two very small occasional seats.

The FHC model was more radically altered. The bulkhead was completely different from the other models in that it was re-designed to enclose the engine sides. In other words, the footwells protruded forward either side of the engine. The windscreen line was moved forward slightly and these changes gave considerably more legroom. The front wings were therefore shorter and the doors longer than other XK140 models.

Interior space was further increased by moving the rear of the roof line back by 6½in and headroom improved by raising the line by 1½in. Additionally, the rear bulkhead was altered to fit small extra seats in the rear as on the DHC. The FHC retained two six volt batteries, but these were mounted in a 'battery box' in each front wing. The body colour bonnet stay was mounted on the bonnet on this model, as opposed to the inner wings on the other models.

The OTS bulkhead, which was raised by 1in, was also moved forward a little and the front wings now had the square return at the 'A' post in the manner of the FHC and DHC 120s and 140s, although the top external line was still angled. This model did not have the occasional rear seats.

above
In right-hand drive form the XK140 roadster is an extremely rare car: only 73 were produced, and just 47 stayed in Britain. Today left-hand drive cars are being imported into Britain and converted to right-hand drive.

right
In left-hand drive form the XK140 roadster was extremely popular in the USA and comfortably outsold the other models.

opposite, top
The bumper does rather dominate the front view of the XK140 in comparison with the XK120's skimpy bumper.

opposite, bottom
Although the XK140's rear bumpers were the same larger section as the front bumper, at least they were restricted to two smaller quarter sections, each carrying an overrider.

BODY TRIM

The most obvious external difference between 120s and 140s was the replacement of the former's delicate bumpers with very much larger items. The front bumper was a single one-piece, double-fluted, chromed item and the rear sprouted two quarter bumpers of the same section. Pairs of overriders were mounted front and rear.

The grille was now a cast one, rather heavier in appearance with seven integral slats. An enamel badge was fixed to the top centre of the grille. From this point a chrome bead ran down the centre of the bonnet. A similar bead, or motif bar, ran down the bootlid and incorporated another enamel badge. This line was continued by the plunger-type boot handle, a short length of bead and the cast 'goose-neck' holder for the combined reversing and number plate light. The headlamp rims are not interchangeable with the 120, those on the 140 being deeper. A simple straight chrome bead was added to the top of the number plate plinth.

The bonnet strip, bumpers, overriders, badges, motif bars, lever-type door handles (the same as the 120 DHC), boot handles, goose necks, headlamp rims, spears, number plate lights, grilles, and number plate beads are all available today. A chrome trim surrounds the windscreen, and this is an expensive hand-made item today. All seals are available.

The grille used on the Jaguar Mark I saloon is very similar to a 140 one, but not identical. The 140 grille has a

left
The XK120's grille was expensive to manufacture, which would never have suited William Lyons. Probably for this reason the 140 has a cast grille.

above
The XK140's enamel badge (like all the badges this is available today) was mounted on a flat section of the grille top with a single stud fixing.

top right
All XK models have what are known as 'spears' on top on the headlamp pods. They are interchangeable between all models and available today. The 140 OTS windscreen assembly remained unchanged from that of the 120. Unfortunately the cast pillars are often badly pitted today, but if these blemishes cannot be polished out prior to rechroming, at least new items are on the market once more.

far right
Although the fuel filler had been fitted in a lower position on XK120 DHC models as a result of the hood design, the position was standardised on the 140s.

near right, above
The exterior door handles used on the XK140 DHC are very different from those of the XK140 FHC, but identical to those fitted to the XK120 DHC.

near right, below
Whereas the XK120's combined reversing light and number plate was carried on a simple fabricated metal bracket, the 140 assembly was fixed to a cast item known as a 'goose neck'. The whole of this light should be chrome-plated, including the rear body.

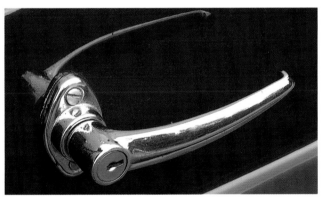

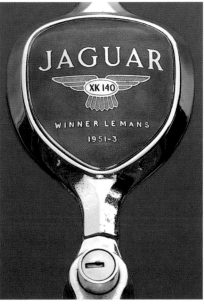

plain area at the top with a single small hole – on the Mark I the badge is fitted from behind.

Owing to its large roof, the FHC's rear quarter lights and rear window were correspondingly larger than the 120's. The doors on this model had exterior handles of the plunger-type, which are available today and interchangeable with those on the 150s. The screen chrome trims are not currently obtainable.

The OTS windscreen assembly was unchanged from that of the 120, and is thus interchangeable.

LIGHTS

The XK140's headlamps were changed and recognisable by a small 'J' on a black circular background mounted in the centre of the lens. A variety of different types were fitted depending on the market to which the car was being supplied. A few cars had an upright rectangular 'J' badge.

New, separate flashers with amber lenses were fitted to the most forward extremities of the front wings for most markets. New rear lamps – incorporating a reflector flasher and stop and tail lamps in one unit – were adopted. Special Equipment cars were fitted with two fog lamps mounted on the front bumper valance panels.

XK140 flashers were fitted to Mark II and Mark VII/IX Jaguars, and the rear lamps to certain models of London taxi. The lenses were also used on the D-type, XK-SS, Triumph Spitfire Mark I, Austin Healey Sprite Mark I and Series 2 MM 1954–55 Morris Minor. All the lights are available today.

CHASSIS

The XK140's chassis was altered in a number of detail ways. The chassis members no longer 'kicked up' at the front to take the front bumpers. Instead the main box members concluded at the front with a flat top plane and a small fabricated section curved round to join the two ends. The engine mountings were revised, because the engine was moved 3in forwards, and the rear cross bracing altered. The rearmost tubular crossmember now sat on top of the chassis legs rather than between them. The crossmember just forward of this point was altered to take the top mountings of the different shock absorbers, and brackets were added to the chassis where it sweeps up. Two holes were now provided in the main central crossmember for the twin exhaust (when fitted).

above
The integral sidelight housings were identical to those which appeared during the life of the XK120. They are a separate pressing which is welded to the wing and then lead loaded over. This area is a good indication of body condition, for if the pressing has lifted, or there are a few bubbles in the paint, there is probably extensive corrosion throughout the body.

left
XK140s were fitted with separate flashers, or indicators, on the front, and these carried the familiar amber lens, except in some countries (such as France) which specified white.

FRONT SUSPENSION

The Special Equipment XK120's uprated torsion bars were fitted as standard equipment to the 140s. Specification details are as follows: castor angle, 1½° to 2° positive; camber angle, ½° to 1° positive; swivel inclination, 5°; wheel alignment (toe-in), parallel to ⅛in toe-in.

Otherwise the front suspension remained unchanged. Hub bearings, all bushes, ball joints and shock absorbers (Spax or Koni) are available today.

REAR SUSPENSION

The lever-arm type rear shock absorbers of the XK120s were replaced by telescopic items. They were manufactured by Girling and their part number was CDR.7/1ONF. Rear shock absorbers (Koni or Spax) are available today, as are the necessary rubber mountings.

BRAKES

The tandem master cylinder adopted during the life of the XK120 was dropped in favour of the original single type for the 140s. Wheel cylinders, master cylinders, hoses, handbrake cables and shoes are all available today.

STEERING

This was an area of more major change with the fitment of Alford and Alder rack and pinion, which gave a lighter steering feel. This was mounted to the chassis by a 'sandwich' of two metal plates with rubber bonded between. The use of two of these mountings helped to absorb vibration. With the scuttle raised slightly, the wheel could be mounted a little higher, and the use of a universal joint in the column presented it more vertically to the driver. The wheel was 1in smaller than the 120's, and the same as the 150's. Steering wheels are being manufactured today, as are rack mountings and rubber bellows.

WHEELS

The hub caps fitted to the steel wheels were now entirely chrome-plated and no longer had any body colour element. Wire wheels were available to special order. Likewise, 'rimbellishers' could be ordered for steel wheels. Only chrome-plated wire wheels were listed in the Parts Book, but these were available in body colour as well.

top
Rear flashers were incorporated in new, larger, rear lamps, which also had integral reflectors in anticipation of new legislation enforced in October 1956.

above
Pressed steel wheels on the XK140s were still painted body colour, although the hub caps lost their colour element and were entirely chrome-plated. This car is fitted with the rimbellishers which were an optional extra, and are being made today.

TYRES

Dunlop white wall tyres were now listed as being available to special order, but otherwise tyre specification was unaltered.

INTERIOR TRIM

Moving the scuttle forward enabled the seats to have an extra 3in of travel. All 140 seats had nine flutes as opposed to the variations on 120s. Unless ordered otherwise, the seats were trimmed in a single colour. A panel at the front end of the boot area could now be folded down into the cockpit to allow longer items of luggage, such as golf clubs, to be carried. A small chrome-plated 'door finger pull' was located on top of the wooden trim panel on each door (as on 120 FHCs and DHCs), and the door was opened by sliding a chrome knob rearwards. Both of these items are available today.

The DHC models had the extra small rear seats, which were rather crudely made up of a small cushion resting on the stepped floor between the back axle hump and a pair of back rests between the wheelarches and the hump. As this hump was slightly off-centre, these items were assymetrical. The tops were trimmed in hide and the sides were in moquette. The area below and behind them was covered in Hardura.

above
The three XK140 models followed the interior styles set by their predecessors, and so the DHC had luxurious appointments with much evidence of polished walnut.

opposite
XK140 seats were not identical to those of the 120s, having nine flutes. The door strikers and dovetails are all currently available.

left
Door trim was very similar to earlier models, but the interior door handle became a sliding type located at the top front of the door.

top left
The fly-off handbrake was dropped and a more conventional (but less sporty) press-button type was adopted on the 140.

top
One of the major differences of the new range was the revised rear layout which allowed two small children, or adults without legs, to be carried. The family man could enjoy life a little longer!

above
The three clips used to fasten the hood to the windscreen top rail, plus the pieces they clip to, are all obtainable today, but the chrome beads on the hood are not.

left
To prevent the folded hood from becoming unfolded, long chrome-plated hooks held it down. These parts are being remanufactured today.

opposite
As you can see from this photograph, it was also an advantage if the children did not have legs either! In practice one adult can sit sideways.

left
The bootlid underside is covered in rexine, and in the middle is situated a small lamp. The bootlid stay clips up to this underside area and a small metal disc prevents the end of the stay damaging the fabric.

below
The bootlid on the XK140s stops shorter than that of the 120s, and there is a fixed panel between the tonneau sections which takes the number plate plinth; a PVC body colour bead lies between the plinth and bootlid. The boot floor is covered by a one-piece Hardura mat.

opposite
The wooden boot floor hinges up and is held open by a small leather strap on the underside of the bootlid. Situated on the underside of the boot floor are the jack with black rubber socket and clip, the ratchet which is held by a Terry's 1162 fixing clip, the wheelbrace (four Terry's 80/0 clips) and the grease gun (two Terry's 1195/1 clips.).

The wheelarches, hump and boot access panel were covered in moquette.

The top rail above the windscreen was covered internally in headlining material. An adjustable interior mirror was fitted and is available today. The hood, when folded, was retained in position by chrome-plated long metal hooks attached to the wheelarch tops, and these are available. The boot floor was covered in a Hardura mat with small black-headed studs. The sides and end panel were also covered in Hardura, and rexine was used on the underside of the bootlid. The original texture pattern of Hardura is no longer available.

The FHC shared these changes, but its additional small rear seats were slightly different from those of the DHC in having a deeper front which lipped over the stepped floor. A few early cars had rear seat backs which were very much taller and stretched almost to the top of the hinged flap. Green Perspex sun visors were fitted.

The OTS model lacked the occasional rear seats but did have the extra seat travel of the other models. The area behind the seats was covered in Hardura.

top left
The FHC interior followed the familiar lines of the coupé models, but had longer footwells protruding either side of the engine. The indicator switch on the dash is incorrect, as are the tacho and speedo.

left
The FHC also had 'pygmy seats' and, like other 140 models, a fold-down flap gave access to the boot area to allow long objects to be carried. Greater glass area gave a more airy feel to the 140 FHC, which was perhaps the most practical XK yet.

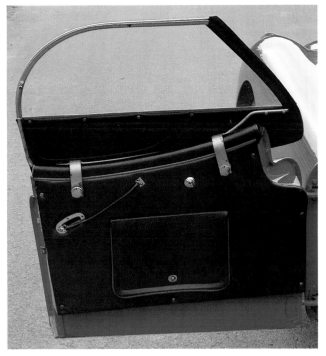

above
The general layout of the XK140 OTS closely followed that of its forerunner, including the cockpit rolls to door tops, scuttle and tonneau panels. Although it is possible that a customer could have ordered a car with contrasting seat piping, it was certainly not usual.

left
In this photograph the red piping again should be ignored; the door pull is also too short and should be like the 120's seen earlier. However, one way in which this car quite correctly differs from the 120 is that the bottom panel, which mates with the sill on closing, was left untrimmed.

ELECTRICS

The horn push in the centre of the steering wheel was now a virtually flat one as fitted to late 120s. A distributor suppressor was added to 140s. One type of fuse box cover was fitted to the open cars and another type to the closed model.

Most electrical items can be reconditioned and the fuse boxes are available today.

TRANSMISSION

Laycock de Normanville overdrive was offered as an optional extra on 140s, as was Borg-Warner automatic transmission on late FHC and DHC models.

DASHBOARD AND INSTRUMENTS

The XK140 differed from the 120 in detail ways. The indicator control was placed on the dashboard in the centre top position. An interior light operated by a dashboard switch was now fitted to the DHC. Cars fitted with fog lamps had an extra light switch position, and the instrument panel assembly had a different part number. Overdrive models had a small transparent illuminated switch, mounted adjacent to the column.

The red line on the 140's tachometer rose by 300rpm to 5500rpm. Otherwise all the instruments were the same and thus interchangeable.

Like the DHC, the FHC continued to have a traditional walnut veneer dashboard. The roadster's dashboard continued to be leather covered, but whereas the central dash panel on the 120 was raked that on the 140 OTS was vertical, with curved sides. The indicator control was placed to the right of the steering column on right-hand drive OTS models.

ENGINE

The uprated Special Equipment 180/190bhp engine used in the 120s was adopted as standard for the 140s. This had ⅜in-lift cams and the head was painted green. The C-type head was available to order and in this form the engine produced 210bhp. The C-type head was painted red on 140s, and small red identifying badges were added to its cam covers soon after introduction; early C-type head 140s did not have these badges.

opposite
The 140 DHC dashboard varied from 120 practice in a few small details. The sides of the centre panel were curved, the tacho's red line began at higher revs, and there were two bronze coloured ashtrays instead of one on top of the dash. The 'arrow head' switch situated at top centre operated the indicators, and the small drawer, which was silk flock lined, could be used for storage or removed for fitment of a radio.

top
We have to be super-critical to fault this photograph! The coil should strictly have a Lucas transfer on it (these are actually being produced again in the USA) and the top hose should be fabric covered.

above left
XK140 engine compartments (and the bonnet undersides) were painted body colour. Most of the parts seen in this photograph are correct, which is surprisingly hard to find today.

above right
The vitreous enamelled exhaust manifolds can clearly be seen in this photograph. This engine thankfully does not suffer from being 'over-bulled'. Many owners make the mistake, as far as originality is concerned, of making their cars smarter than new. There is nothing worse to the true enthusiast that an excess of non-standard chromed items.

above
The roadster shown here has the earlier, plain-topped radiator, but rather more modern pancake air filters. The HT leads should run over the front of the head and be located by a chrome ring connector. This engine has the very desirable C-type head; the head is painted red and cam covers bear the special badges. This head came to be offered on road cars because someone ordered a thousand of the castings for the racing cars by mistake!

right
This DHC is fitted with the later radiator, which has fluting on the header tank. The radiator cap is a more modern addition.

CARBURETTORS

Two SU H6 1¾in carburettors, as fitted to later 120s, were used on the standard 140s. A large circular drum type air cleaner assembly made by AC Delco (7222695), with the air cleaner element at the front of it, was fitted to all 140s with the standard cylinder head. This connected to the carburettors via a rather stylish aluminium cast air intake pipe. A pair of pancake-type air cleaners (AC Delco 1579565) were used on the OTS and DHC models when fitted with C-type cylinder head and 1¾in carburettors. A different air cleaner (1572943), although presumably still pancake type, was fitted to all 140s with the C-type head and 2in carbs.

COOLING SYSTEM

XK140s had a different radiator, which was raked to avoid the new steering rack. Four patterns of radiator were fitted at different times. Early cars had a flat-topped, square pattern radiator, rather than the later fluted pattern illustrated here. Early ones had two tie-bars down to the chassis, whereas later cars had two tie-bars to the inner wings. A metal eight-bladed fan was fitted and shrouded by a cowl to its sides and bottom.

All hoses are available and radiators can be re-cored if necessary.

EXHAUST

A single system was fitted as standard and this emerged to the left of the number plate. Special Equipment models were fitted with a twin system which ran through the two holes in the main central crossmember and emerged under each overrider – the last 9in of the pipes were chromed.

Exhaust systems in either steel or stainless steel (unoriginal of course) are available today.

PRODUCTION CHANGES

Chassis numbers refer to RHD/LHD

Feb 1955
From: Engine No. G.1908
Rotor type oil pump and circular oil seal adopted at front end of the crankshaft. Oil pressure relief valve fitted in the filter head.

Mar 1955
From: OTS 800022/81193
     FHC 804031/814053
     DHC 807047/817268
On 4.09:1 ratio rear axles fitted to XK140 overdrive cars, flat drive gear bolt lockstraps are incorporated.

Jun 1955
From: G.3250 (and certain earlier engines)
For Special Equipment cars with C-type head, standard carburettor and disc air cleaners, the recommended carburettor needles are changed from SL to WO2.

From: OTS 800031/811382
     FHC 804121/814216
     DHC 807113/817426
Relay incorporated in the electrical circuit for the operation of overdrive.

All engines:
'On cars with pressed steel sumps it is not desirable to have the level of oil above the top mark on the dipstick when the engine is hot and therefore oil level checks and topping up of engine oil should be undertaken when the engine is *hot* and not when the engine is cold as has previously been our recommendation'.

From: OTS 800025/811284
     FHC 804080/814153
     DHC 807080/817356
Altered rear brake wheel cylinders (Part No. 39677) adopted.

From: FHC 804020/814035
Radiator C.7523, Mounting Bracket C.8830, 16in fan (as opposed to 15½in) adopted.

From: OTS 800037/811424
     FHC 804124/814241
     DHC 807128/817460
Radiator C.9619, Mounting Bracket C.8830

Sep 1955
From: Engine No. G.4431 (plus 4411 to 4420)
Spring-loaded Renold chain tensioner (C.10332) adopted in place of spring blade type of lower timing chain tensioner. Nylon damper assembly (C.10290) fitted in position originally occupied by the guide bracket for the spring blade type of tensioner. Block altered to provide oil feed to timing chain via tensioner.

From: OTS 800052/811562
     FHC 804308/814532
     DHC 807237/817653
Castor angle altered from 2½ – 3° positive to 1½ – 2° positive to remedy 'steering kick'.

Dec 1955

From: Engine No. G.5789
Modified cylinder head adopted with reduced depth of tapped holes for studs on the inlet face.

From: Engine No. G.6233
Modified oil filter adopted – identifiable by head or centre bolt being at the bottom henceforth.

Identification of 5½K pressed steel wheels by two depressions adjacent to valve hole dispensed with. '5½K' stamped in well of wheel rim.

From: OTS 800062/811866
FHC 804523/815252
DHC 807319/818393
Overdrive cars: throttle switch incorporated in the electrical operation of the overdrive. Two relays fitted and wiring harness modified.

Apr 1956

From: Engine No. G.7229
Piston rings with tapered periphery compression rings and modified oil control rings adopted.

From: Standard Transmission OTS 800071/812311
FHC 804676/815528
DHC 807389/818488
Bolts which secure the drive gear to the differential case increased from ⅜in (9.5mm) to 7/16in (11mm).

Sep 1956

From: OTS 800072/812647
FHC 804767/815755
DHC 807441/818729
'Fly-off' handbrake adopted.

Oct 1956

From: FHC 804781/815773
DHC 807447/818796
Steel doors adopted rather than aluminium.

Feb 1957

Steel cylinder head gasket (C.7891) adopted in place of Klingerite (C.2250) and cupro-nickel (C.3335).

Jan 1958

Brake servo kit available.

SPECIAL EQUIPMENT SPECIFICATION

Wire Spoke Wheels with Splined Hubs and Knock-On Hub Caps
Pair of Lucas FT 576 Fog Lamps.

OPTIONAL EXTRAS

"Note: items under this heading are supplied only when specially ordered."
Windscreen Washer Assembly (for use only on OTS and DHC).
Windscreen Washer Assembly (for use only on FHC).
Control Button Assembly on instrument panel for windscreen washers.
Connection in inlet manifold for tube to control button.
Wire Spoke Road Wheel (chromium plated)
Tyre (Dunlop Racing 6.00in x 16in).
Inner Tube (to suit).
Tyre (Dunlop White Wall).
Rimbellisher.
Tool for removal of hub discs.
External Luggage Rack for installation to luggage compartment lid.
Fog Lamp (Lucas 55128/B–SFT.576) (for all countries except France).
Fog Lamp (Lucas 55133/B–SFT.576) (for export to France).
Brackets for mounting fog lamps.
Switch operating fog lamps (replaces standard lamp switch on instrument panel).
Laycock de Normanville Overdrive.
Borg-Warner Automatic Transmission (later).

COLOUR SCHEMES

COACHWORK	INTERIOR OTS	FHC	DHC	HOOD OTS	DHC
Black	Red Biscuit and Red two-tone	Red Tan Grey Biscuit	Red Tan Grey Biscuit	Black	Black Sand
Birch Grey	Red Biscuit and Red two-tone	Red Blue Grey	Red Grey Pale Blue	French Grey Black	French Grey Black
Pastel Green	Suede Green	Suede Green	Suede Green Grey	Fawn Black	Fawn Black
Pearl Grey	Red Blue Grey	Red Blue Grey	Red Blue Grey	Blue Black French Grey	Blue Black French Grey
Pacific Blue	Blue Grey	Blue Grey	Blue Grey	Blue Black	Blue Black
British Racing Green	Tan Suede Green	Tan Suede Green	Tan Suede Green	Gunmetal Black	Gunmetal Black
Dove Grey	Tan Biscuit	Tan Biscuit	Tan Biscuit	Fawn Sand Black	Fawn Sand Black
Suede Green	Suede Green	Suede Green	Suede Green	French Grey Black	French Grey Black
Red	Red Biscuit and Red two-tone	Red	Red	Fawn Black	Fawn Black
Lavender Grey	Red Suede Green Pale Blue	Red Suede Green	Red Suede Green Pale Blue	Fawn Black	Fawn Black
Battleship Grey	Red Biscuit and Red two-tone	Red Grey	Red Grey Biscuit	Gunmetal Black	Gunmetal Black
Cream	Red Biscuit and Red two-tone	Red	Red Pale Blue	Fawn Black Blue	Fawn Black Blue
Pastel Blue	Light and Dark Blue two-tone Blue	Light Blue	Light Blue	French Grey Black Blue	French Grey Black Blue
Maroon	Red Biscuit	Red Biscuit	Red Biscuit	Black Sand	Black Sand

CHASSIS NUMBERS/DATES

Model	Years Manufactured	Chassis Numbers RHD	LHD
Open Two-Seater (OTS)	1954–1957	800001	810001
Fixed Head Coupé (FHC)	1954–1957	804001	814001
Drophead Coupé (DHC)	1954–1957	807001	817001

'A' prefix to chassis number indicates Special Equipment model.
'S' prefix indicates SE model with C-type cylinder head.
'DN' suffix indicates fitment of overdrive.

/7, /8 or /9 suffix indicates compression ratio.

Engine Numbers commence: G.1001.   In USA: XK140 SE known as XK140M; XK140 SE with C-type head known as XK140MC.

XK150

BODY

The method of construction of the XK150 body was very similar to that of the 140, but most panels were rather different in shape.

The most obvious change was to the wing line. Whereas it had swept in such exaggerated fashion on the previous models, the wing shape was comparatively straight on the 150s. The front wings differed, and additionally the lip which

turned up to meet the bonnet was deleted. This enabled the bonnet to be widened, by inserting a 4in fillet down its centre.

Much slimmer doors increased interior width. The rear wings continued the straighter line. A revised bumper layout necessitated moving the number plate plinth, which became an integral part of the lower portion of the bootlid. On earlier 150s this plinth protruded further from the bootlid line at the top than on later cars; in other words the number plate was nearer to the vertical, as required initially by American regulations. This plinth was a separate panel welded to the steel bootlid and leaded over.

opposite
The XK150 was very different from its predecessors. The most obvious change was the considerable straightening of the wing line.

above
The appearance was modernised significantly by the adoption of a one-piece windscreen, and the 4in wider bonnet made it far easier to work on the engine. The situation was still far from ideal, but an American mechanic was now less likely to say: 'I'd fix it, if I could find it'!

left
Chris Fletcher's XK150 FHC, an exceptionally original car.

above
It is easy to see that the XK150 was an ageing concept in the late 1950s, but then the basic design had been in production for around ten years.

right
As the last manifestation of the concept, the XK150 was the most sophisticated. It was another step in the softening process that had started with the 140, and would continue after the 150.

below
While the XK150 was a little old-fashioned in the late fifties with its separate chassis and live rear axle, performance was gradually boosted. The car benefitted from the real advantage and prestige of having the 'new' disc brakes.

top right
The DHC was introduced, like the FHC, in May 1957, but only one reached the home market that year and just 160 were exported. This example is owned by John Schofield.

right
The XK150 DHC was always outsold by the FHC, but less so as time passed. As with all XKs, a high proportion, some 75%, was exported.

far right
A confusing array of engine options gradually became available during the life of the XK150, with the ultimate 3.8-litre triple carburettor version being introduced near the end. It was clearly intended for something rather different in the way of exciting sports cars . . .

Earlier cars had a tubular strut to hold up the bootlid, but this was superseded by a simple stay similar to those on 120s and 140s. This arrangement in turn was replaced by sprung hinges which cause the boot to raise itself when opened, catching unwary people under the chin.

The only body panels which are interchangeable with 140s are the boot and spare wheel well panels plus the rear lower panel, occasional seat area and centre floor section. The hinged plywood boot floor was covered on its top side with sheet aluminium painted black.

The OTS 150 also had its scuttle moved 4in rearwards. As a result, the bonnet was longer and there was a 'step' in the 'A' post line. Consequently the doors are not interchangeable with the other models. Otherwise, most 150 panels are interchangeable between the three body styles, and all panels are being remanufactured today.

top
The XK150 roadster was introduced 10 months after the other models, in March 1958. In what was left of that year it out-sold the other two models on the export market and clearly justified the eventual decision to produce it.

above left
Like the earlier roadsters, the XK150 version was strictly a two-seater, but the archaic side screens had now gone to be replaced by rather more modern wind-up windows. Peter Walker owns this car.

top left
Only a handful of XK150 roadsters were sold in Britain, and none reached the market until November 1958, when just one standard example and one 'S' were released into British hands.

above
The edges around the wheelarch and along the bottom of the wing are wired; the sheet steel is rolled over a piece of steel wire. This area is a haven for corrosion and will need replacing on many cars.

opposite
The scuttle on the roadster was actually moved back 4in to reduce interior space as there would otherwise have been an embarrassment of room behind the seats. As a result the rear tonneau panel seemed almost excessively long. The rearward move of the scuttle necessitated a step in the 'A' post line, akin to the later E-type.

BODY TRIM

The front bumper was altered to include a dish in the centre under the grille. At the rear the two quarter bumpers were replaced by a single wraparound item. On later cars the overriders were moved inwards to within the bootlid line, whereas on earlier cars they were positioned at the extremities, under the rear lights. A new broader grille was fitted to the wider bonnet and it was now more akin to the 120's construction.

The rapidly dating two-piece windscreen was replaced by a single piece wraparound screen surrounded by chrome-plated trim. Plunger-type exterior door handles were fitted on all models. The car's appearance – and the driver's rear view – was improved by a larger rear window.

All bootlid chrome trim was altered as a result of moving the number plate. A deeper section motif bar ran down from the top of the bootlid and incorporated a circular badge, below which was the bootlid's plunger-type handle. On earlier cars the rearmost end of this handle finished above the lip on the number plate plinth. Later cars had a rubber pad, resting on top of the chrome number plate lamp assembly, added to the handle. This assembly ran across the top of the plinth and had chrome-plated trims along each side of the square number plate.

All these pieces of body trim are interchangeable with other 150s, and the bootlid items, top and bottom screen

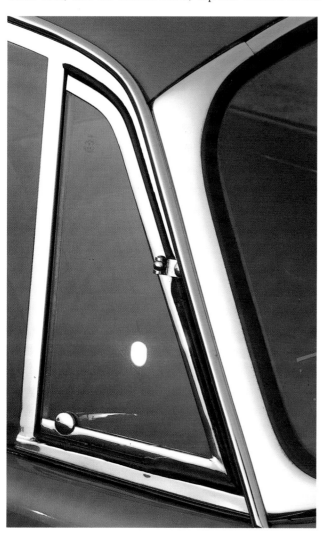

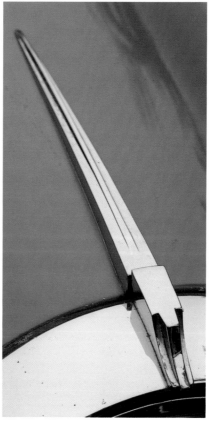

above
The XK150 front remained very much in the Jaguar theme. It had a wider and more delicate grille than the 140, and the front bumper was given a little more style with a depression under the grille. Note fillet inserted into bonnet to widen it.

far left
Like the earlier models, the XK150 FHC and DHC had a useful source of ventilation from their front quarterlights. The windscreen chrome side trims are not currently available, but it will only be a matter of time before someone remanufactures them.

left
The headlamps rims, spears and little motif on top of the rims are all as fitted to 140s, and available today.

opposite
There is no bonnet safety catch on 150s and the bonnet can flex, fly up and strike the roof, or the unfortunate driver in the case of open cars. Sadly this happened to this car soon after it had been photographed. While it is highly unoriginal, it is very sensible to thread a small leather strap around the base of the grille and the panel below.

chrome trims and the bonnet strip are available today. The bonnet badge and the chrome trim into which it fits at the top of the grille are being re-manufactured. This grille is almost identical to a 3.4 Mark I – the only way to identify the XK150 item is by the safety catch at the bottom. The chrome guttering trim is also now being made.

'S' models were identifiable by small chrome-plated 'S' badges positioned at the front of the door tops. These were handed, and are available.

The DHC model had additional chrome beads to the hood and surround – these are difficult to obtain. DHC window frames differed and obviously no rear quarterlights were fitted. The OTS gained wind-up windows in a simple frame without quarterlights.

above
The top and bottom windscreen chrome trims are now available, but the bonnet trim is not. The step in the roadster front door line is noticeable here.

top right
The rear window continued to grow with each model, reflecting more modern thinking. The two rear quarter bumpers of the 140s were now gone, replaced by a single, hefty wraparound item. Curiously, the fuel filler cap on the 150s opened in the opposite direction to those fitted to the earlier cars. Obtaining front and rear screens presents no problems today. All the side windows are flat.

right
The rear number plate arrangement was completely revised on the 150s and incorporated a square plate, probably in deference to American requirements.

far right
The motif bar and badge, which now included mention of three further Le Mans wins, were different from those on the 140, but, like all bootlid trim items, they are manufactured again today.

LIGHTS

XK150s used the same headlamps, sidelights and front flashers as 140s. The rear lamps also remained unchanged until larger units with separate amber indicators and reflectors were introduced for later cars. The combined reversing and number plate light was a completely different part from that of previous models. As with the 150's predecessors, there were some variations for foreign markets. For example, cars bound for Switzerland had clear lenses in the front flashers – these being wired as sidelights while the normal sidelights were used as flashers.

All these items are interchangeable between 150 models and are available today.

CHASSIS

The 150's chassis had an additional body mounting bracket on each side, and the curved section joining the two main members at the front was removed. The petrol pump was now mounted outboard on the right-hand side of the chassis behind the sill.

FRONT SUSPENSION

The 150's front suspension was exactly the same as the 140's.

opposite
The headlamps and sidelights remained as used on the 140s. The leaping Jaguar mascot became an optional extra for the first time on an XK, but the fitment has often caused some damage to the surrounding area of the bonnet as people have, over the years, opened and closed the bonnet with the mascot, exerting a strain on the adjacent area. The badge bar is a period extra.

above
Later 150s had a different, larger rear lamp with an amber indicator and separate reflector below the rear lights. Also on later cars the overriders were moved closer together.

below left
During discussions with experts in the preparation of this book, there was much lengthy, but hilarious, debate on one point of the utmost gravity – which way round should the red sidelight tell-tales be? Eventually, with reputations at stake, a vote was taken and the unique gathering of XK expertise found in favour of the manner illustrated here.

below right
The combined tail, stop and indicator rear lights with integral reflectors were, until later in production, the same as those used on the 140s. These units can still be seen on older versions of the current London taxi cab.

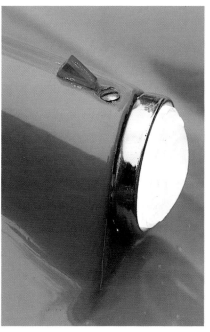

79

REAR SUSPENSION

The rear suspension was also unchanged, but 'S' models had nine leaves (instead of seven). All should still have gaiters and grease nipples.

STEERING

The 150's steering wheel and horn push are interchangeable with the 140s. The wheels, track rod ends, rack mountings, rubber bellows and rubber cross coupling are all obtainable. Racks can be rebuilt.

BRAKES

It was in braking that XK150s made great advances over their predecessors. In place of the barely adequate traditional drum brakes, the 150s adopted all-round disc brakes, which had been developed on the C-type and D-type.

Each disc employed a single caliper housing a pair of round pads. These calipers worked hydraulically by means of a master cylinder with Lockheed vacuum servo assistance. Power was received for its operation from atmospheric pressure and by vacuum from the engine inlet manifold via a vacuum tank. The servo was mounted in a most inaccessible position in the nearside front wing and had its own air cleaner – this rarely receives attention, to the detriment of the servo assistance.

The handbrake continued to be mechanically operated and was connected to the rear brake calipers which carried independent pads and separate adjustment.

In May 1959 the round pad calipers were replaced by a new design allowing the use of quick-change square pads.

Many cars have since been converted to this more practical set-up. The round pads can still be obtained, although they are old stock. It is questionable whether re-manufacture will be feasible when this stock is exhausted. Hoses, caliper piston kits, seals, master cylinders, pads, discs and handbrake cables are available today.

WHEELS

The vast majority of 150s were produced in Special Equipment form with wire wheels. From June 1958, 54-spoke wheels were replaced by 60-spoke wheels.

INTERIOR TRIM

XK150 seats were slightly wider as a result of the shallower doors, and their squabs were thinner to improve rear legroom. The rear wheelarches were a different shape and enclosed by a casing generally covered in moquette, although some DHCs have been known with rexine. The rear parcel shelf on the FHCs was covered in moquette. The rear occasional seats were the same width as those of the 140s.

The doors had a large map pocket running the length of the door and, on earlier cars, solid armrests. From May 1958 these were hollowed out to double as a door pull. The interior door handles worked on the same principle as those of the 140s but were dimensionally different. Some cars had ashtrays at the bottom of the doors below the door handles – otherwise the ashtray was positioned on the transmission tunnel, and some had a small leaping mascot on the top. Roadster door casings and top rolls were different from the other models.

The boot materials were as for the 140, but the small circular cut-outs in the boot floor Hardura mat for the locking mechanism were fitted with large rubber grommets.

far left
The steering wheel and 'flat' horn push from the 140s continued to be used, and both are once more available today.

left
The 16in wire wheels could be supplied in chrome plate or Dunlop Wheel Silver as required, or in body colour to special order. The vast majority of 150s were fitted with wire wheels, but those few cars with pressed steel wheels still left the factory with spats.

right
In an effort to assist the unfortunate rear seat passengers, the front seat squabs were made rather slimmer, but otherwise the rear arrangement was relatively unaltered.

below
XK interiors became increasingly more civilised, and the 150 benefitted in terms of interior width from considerably slimmer doors.

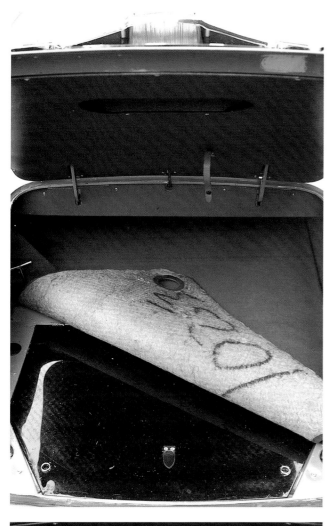

opposite, top
The XK150 rear quarterlights opened in the usual way. The Furflex trim used here and on other parts of the car is available today in a wide range of colours.

opposite, bottom left
XK150 doors were given larger pockets and a new chrome trim strip. The door handles operated in the same way as the 140's but are not interchangeable. The car shown here, a later version, has a combined armrest and door pull, as opposed to the solid armrest of very early cars.

opposite, bottom right
The rear panel above the occasional seats continued to be hinged for access to the boot from inside, providing the ability to carry, for example, a set of golf clubs. The shape of the inner wings changed on the 150s.

above left
The boot arrangement was similar to that on the 140s, and indeed several of the panels are interchangeable. The opening on the underside of the bootlid trim allowed the number plate light to shine through and illuminate the boot area. On 150s the boot floor mat has rubber grommets around the cut-outs for the locking mechanism.

left
The layout of tools on the underside of the boot floor was as before. The boot floor was locked down in place by two coach locks operated by the 'T' bar which lived on the petrol filler pipe cover.

above right
Being a wire wheel car, this 150 is equipped with a Thor copper/hide hammer for use on the spinners, as well as the comprehensive tool roll. The spare wheel bolt 'dish' is the other way up on a 150. The spare wheel well extension is incorrectly body colour on the car seen here; it should be black, which the jack should not! That should be red on all cars.

left
The interior of the XK150 DHC followed the same lines as the 140 DHC and 150 FHC. You can clearly see here the high standard of luxury provided by the complex lined hood.

above
The DHC hood was clipped down when in the folded position in the same manner as the 140 before it, but these clips are not interchangeable.

top right
The relative crudeness of the roadster hood can be seen, with the hood sticks clearly visible to the occupants, as on most open cars. The rear window could still be unzipped.

bottom right
The roadster hood, which like all the others was made from mohair, can be supplied today by specialist trimmers, and the hood frames are believed to be available in the USA. The chrome bead is not obtainable.

top left
The XK150 roadster has a useful amount of space behind the rear seats, where the two extra seats would be on the other models. To lower the hood, one first folded back the short, trimmed tonneau panel extension.

top right
Having released the catches on the top rail above the windscreen, and slid the rear of the hood off the 'tear drops' on the tonneau panel, the hood was lifted and folded back.

above
The operation of lowering the hood was completed by carefully folding it down behind the seats. The tonneau extension could then be locked back in place to conceal the hood neatly.

right
A tonneau cover was supplied and clipped to the rear tonneau extension at the back, and at the front it clipped into the demister vents.

top

Apart from a few early cars, XK150 dashboards were leather covered on all three models, and hence rather different from the previous coupés. The outer panels and top roll matched the seats.

above

The centre section of the dash was covered in grey leather. On 120s and 140s the rev counter operated anti-clockwise, but not so on the 150s. Additionally, some cars had an electric rev counter driven via a generator off the back of the cam covers. These are distinguishable by the lack of figures on the clock face, as seen here. Also, the car shown, being a late car, has heater slide controls and an indicator stalk on the column.

right

The overdrive switch, when appropriate, was fitted at the extreme end of the driver's side of the dash, and was a different type of switch from that employed on the 140s.

DASHBOARD AND INSTRUMENTS

The central dashboard on a few early cars was made in aluminium with raised 'little dash' finish. Thereafter the dashboard on all models was covered in hide with the centre panel in grey and the two side panels in seat colour. The three areas making up this panel were edged in chrome bead. Above the dash was a padded roll, and below this in the centre sat the indicator switch (on earlier cars). From June 1958, this function moved to a stalk on the steering column. Later cars fitted with a fresh air heating system had a slide control in the top centre of the dash.

The dash tops were the same on the DHC and FHC models, but shallower on the roadster.

ENGINE

Initially two versions of the XK engine were available, and later several more. The standard car used the 140 engine, but Special Equipment models were fitted with an engine incorporating the newly developed B-type cylinder head. Painted light blue, this head used the 1⅝in exhaust valves from the C-type head, convex valve faces and inlet valve angles altered from 30° to 45°. Power output in this form was 210bhp (like the C-type), but this figure and increased torque were developed at lower revs.

Coinciding with the introduction of the OTS model, an 'S' version was added to the entire range. The 'S' was fitted with what has come to be known as the 'straight port head', painted gold. With straighter ports, a different arrangement of carburettors and inlet manifold, 9:1 pistons, lead bronze bearings and lightened flywheel, power increased to 250bhp.

The range was further supplemented by the introduction of a 3.8–litre version of the XK engine supplied with the B-type head or the 'straight port head'. In the former guise it produced 220bhp and was recognisable from its metallic blue head. In the ultimate version, with gold head, the engine produced a claimed 265bhp. In fact all these power outputs should be taken with a large pinch of salt!

CARBURETTORS

The 'S' versions of the 3.4 and 3.8–litre engines used three 2in SU carburettors. A revised inlet manifold allowed each carburettor to feed a pair of cylinders. A new air cleaner arrangement using air trumpets protruded under the inner front wing on the offside and necessitated some changes to this panel and the battery box on these models.

COOLING SYSTEM

The 150 radiator varied a little from the 140s in that it had a separate filler behind the header tank connected by a short neck. All hoses are available.

EXHAUST

Single and twin systems were fitted.

TRANSMISSION

Manual and automatic transmission cars were fitted with a 3.54:1 axle ratio, while overdrive models had a 4.09:1 ratio. The 'S' models could be ordered with a Powr-Lok limited slip differential.

above
Being a very original car, this FHC's engine compartment has not been 'over-tarted'. Note that the bonnet catch mechanism was moved from the bottom of the opening. This car is fitted with the fresh air heater system which feeds from the wing vent, through trunking, past the heater and into the footwell area.

opposite
As the roadster seen here was restored relatively recently, it is still very glossy in the engine compartment. The bonnet hinges are rather different on the roadster model. Being super-critical, there are one or two incorrect points to be seen here. The carburettor dash tops should not be plastic, the bonnet lock should be body colour, the heater cover should be black and the engine hoist brackets on the head have been fitted later.

Jul 1957

From: Engine No. V.1191
Conical filter gauze (C.13457) fitted to the oil feed hole for the hydraulic chain tensioner in block.

Champion sparking plug designations changed:
L.10.S. (7:1 c/r) now L.7;
N.8.B. (8:1 c/r) now N.8.

Sep 1957

From: Engine No. V.1599
Smaller dynamo pulley adopted to increase dynamo speed. Fan belt shortened to suit.

From: Engine No. V1631
Cylinder block rear cover and sealing ring modified. Allen headed cap screws inserted from top now.

From: FHC 824046/834491
       DHC ——/837030
On automatic cars, anti-creep solenoid adopted.

From: FHC 824023/834454
       DHC ——/837014
Rear brake calipers with 1⅝in (41.3mm) pistons replaced those with 1¾in (44.4mm) pistons.

From: Engine No. V.1281 (plus certain previous)
Longer inlet valves guides adopted.

Nov 1957

From: Engine No. V.2011
Altered oil pressure relief valve adopted. Stop pin fitted in centre of longer and lighter spring, limiting travel of valve.

From: Engine No. V.1921
Timing cover – five bottom set screw hole bosses machined to same length, as opposed to one short and four longer.

From: FHC 824076/834600
       DHC 827001/837071
Altered upper steering column adopted to provide more positive locking of steering wheel.

From: Engine No. V.2029
Synthetic rubber bonded chain dampers adopted in place of nylon type.

From: FHC 824096/834658
       DHC 827001/837090
Fuse nos. 1, 2, 5 & 6 now 50 amp, in place of 35 amp.

From: Automatic transmission units JBX 1001
Now manufactured in England (marked 'Letchworth, Herts, England') rather than USA (marked 'Detroit, Mich, USA').

Feb 1958

Disc brakes – cast iron master cylinder body in place of aluminium.

May 1958

From: FHC 824253/835301
       DHC 827011/837332
Armrest altered to double as door pull.

Jun 1958

Wire wheels with 60 spokes adopted.

From: FHC 824414/835548
       DHC 827069/837415
Indicator switching transferred from dashboard to stalk on steering column.

Jul 1958

From: OTS ——/830439
       FHC 824420/835566
       DHC 827072/837434
Rheostat switch, for variable control of heater motor, adopted and fitted adjacent to rev counter.

From: OTS 820001/830960
       FHC 824551/835671
       DHC 827168/837573
Altered rear spring with thicker top leaf and front spring eye of different design adopted. Also full length interleaf adopted between top and second leaves.

Jan 1959

From: Engine No. V.5733 150 'S' – VS.1523
Fan belt of ½in (12.5mm) width adopted and pulleys altered to suit.

From: OTS 820004/831712
       FHC 824669/835886
       DHC 827236/837836
Bridge type brake calipers with quick change square pads adopted.

From: OTS 820004/831698
       FHC 824668/835882
       DHC 827235/837831
Altered upper wishbone ball joints with larger ball and increased angle of movement adopted.

Apr 1959

From: OTS 820001/831250
       DHC 827209/837662
Rear bumper with less widely spaced overriders adopted.

Jun 1959

From: Engine No. V.6709
Lead indium big end bearings adopted.

From: OTS 820001/830560
       FHC 824453/835589
       DHC 827094/837468
Larger diameter vent tube fitted to petrol tank and new filler box adopted.

From: OTS 820001/830001
      FHC 824677/835893
      DHC 827240/837846
Spring loaded boot lid hinges adopted.

From: Engine No. V.6861
Blanking plate formerly fitted between oil filter and block, deleted. Shorter oil filter bolts used, copper washers only under bolt heads. Joint face of sump cut away to clear oil filter head castings.

Method of securing rev counter gearbox and adaptor to the cylinder head revised. Screws securing adaptor now have nylon insert in the threads.

From: OTS 820014/831825
      FHC 824702/835905
      DHC 827258/837865
Ashtray mounted on transmission tunnel in place of previous position on door.

From: OTS 820001/832071
      DHC 827340/838231
Prismatic interior mirror (C.14920) adopted, replacing plain glass type.

From: FHC 824900/836219
Prismatic interior mirror (C.14900) adopted.
 Windscreen upper panel altered to suit.

From: OTS ———/832088
      FHC 824900/836222
      DHC 827273/838259
25 amp output dynamo and voltage/current regulator with revised current setting adopted.

From: OTS 820038/832674
      FHC 824863/836184
      DHC 827349/838238
Boot lid prop, anchor bracket, spring clip and clip plate deleted. Springs in boot lid re-set to a fully wound condition to retain boot lid in fully open position. Tonneau cross member reinforced.

From: OTS 820039/832076
      FHC 824864/836187
      DHC 827355/838246
XK150 'S' – single air cleaner incorporating paper element adopted in place of three wire mesh type elements.

From: OTS 820043/832089
      FHC 824903/836227
      DHC 827379/838273
Strengthened bracket for mounting of clutch slave cylinder adopted

From: OTS 820043/832089
      FHC 824903/836227
      DHC 827373/838272 (plus certain previous)
Electrically operated rev counter in place of cable type.

From: FHC 824964   150 'S'
Stiffener adopted for spherical bearing support bracket on accelerator cross shaft.

Rear hub oil seal assembly altered to give more efficient sealing condition.

Jul 1959

From: OTS 820017/831899
      FHC 824742/835935
      DHC 827272/837941
Reservac adopted.

Jan 1960

From: Engine Nos. V.7460, VA.1399, VS.2183, VAS.1085
Altered rear cover assembly and cork/rubber seal at rear of block and new oil sump gasket adopted.

From: OTS 820066/932113
      FHC 852125/836635
      DHC 827505/838590
Altered brake master cylinder adopted.

Mar 1960

From: Engine Nos. V.7464, VS.2188
Notched fan belt adopted.

3.8 XK150 'S': cylinder head not chamfered at bottom of combustion chamber, necessitating piston crown of special design to avoid fouling.

From: FHC ———/836724
      DHC 827510/———
Altered connecting link adopted to give improved operation of the handbrake lever.

Apr 1960

From: Engine Nos. V.7496, VA.1708, VS.2197, VAS.1160
Tab washer employed to secure two set screws fixing intermediate chain damper.

From: Engine Nos. V.7524, VS.2195
New 9:1 c/r piston with dome crown adopted.

Overdrive – XK150 3.8: to speed up change into overdrive, lighter clutch springs fitted into overdrive units.

Automatic transmission: altered filler/drain plug and sealing washer adopted on torque convertor.

From: OTS 820071/———
      FHC 825179/836744
      DHC 827540/838754

Warning light adopted which comes into operation when ignition on, if handbrake on or brake fluid low.

Altered facia board adopted to suit above.

Polythene brake fluid container adopted.

Handbrake pads of M.34 material adopted.

Tail pipe no longer welded to silencer but secured by means of a clip.

New rear shock absorber with 1⅜in diameter piston adopted.

May 1960

From: DTS 820071/————
    FHC 825179/836744
    DHC 827540/838754

Mintex M.33 brake pads adopted in place of Ferodo DS.5.

Jun 1960

From: Engine Nos. VA.1882, VAS.1225
Overdrive units fitted with magnetic ring to collect errant metal particles.

Nov 1960

From: Engine Nos. V.7612, VA.2004, VS.2207, VAS.1268
Alterations to rev counter drive to eliminate noise.

From: Engine Nos. V.7640, VA.2054, VAS.1284
Different bearing material adopted.

From: Engine Nos. VA.2053, VAS.1285
Boss provided for fitting of Bray electrical heater moved to right-hand side of block.

Red carpet from: OTS 820069/————
            FHC ————/836687
            DHC ————/838661

Tan carpet from: OTS ————/832118
            FHC 825142/————
            DHC ————/838684

Green carpet from: FHC ————/836731
            DHC 827508/————

Dark blue carpet from: OTS ————/832131
            FHC ————/836765
            DHC 827573/————

Black carpet from: OTS ————/832122
            FHC ————/836827
            DHC ————/838889

Change in quality of carpets introduced in colours listed above. New carpet has straight-cut pile as opposed to curly pile previously.

USA left-hand drive cars from: OTS 832138
FHC 836855 DHC 838904
New headlights adopted to comply with USA Vehicle Lighting Regulations.

Feb 1961

From: Engine Nos. V.7656, VA.2202, VS.2212, VAS.1293
Pressure die-cast timing cover adopted.

From: Engine Nos. V.7656, VA.2204, VS.2212, VAS.1293
Altered small end bearings fitted to connecting rods.

From: Engine No. VA.2251
New studs with longer thread fitted to bottom of timing cover.

From: Engine No. VA.2260
Guide tube fitted to dipstick aperture.

OPTIONAL EXTRAS

Car Radio Assembly (various).

Bucket Seat.

Wing Mirror.

Shield Assembly, protecting sump (fitted as standard equipment on cars exported to certain countries).

Rimbellisher

White-wall Tyre (Dunlop 6.00in x 16in).

Windscreen Glass (anti-glare type).

Jaguar Mascot on bonnet.

Chromium-Plated Moulding (front) at top of bonnet (for use when Jaguar mascot is fitted).

Chromium-Plated Moulding (rear) at top of bonnet (for use when Jaguar mascot is fitted).

Borg-Warner Automatic Transmission.

Laycock de Normanville Overdrive.

SPECIAL EQUIPMENT SPECIFICATION

Wire Spoke Wheels with Splined Hubs and Knock-On Hub Caps
Pair of Lucas Fog Lamps.

COLOUR SCHEMES

COACHWORK	INTERIOR			HOOD	
	OTS	FHC	DHC	OTS	DHC
Pearl Grey	Red Light Blue Dark Blue Grey	Red Light Blue Dark Blue Grey	Red Light Blue Dark Blue Grey	Blue Black French Grey	Blue Black French Grey
Imperial Maroon	Maroon	Maroon	Maroon	Black Sand	Black Sand
Cream	Red	Red	Red Light Blue Dark Blue	Fawn Black Blue	Fawn Black Blue
Indigo Blue	Light Blue Dark Blue Grey	Light Blue Dark Blue Grey	Light Blue Dark Blue Grey	Blue Black	Blue Black
Claret	Red Maroon	Red Maroon	Red Maroon	Black Sand	Black Sand
Cotswold Blue	Dark Blue Grey	Dark Blue Grey	Dark Blue Grey	Blue Black	Blue Black
Black	Red	Red Tan Grey	Red Tan Grey	Black	Black Sand
Mist Grey	Red Light Blue Dark Blue Grey	Red Light Blue Dark Blue Grey	Red Light Blue Dark Blue Grey	French Grey Black	French Grey Black
Sherwood Green	Tan Suede Green	Tan Suede Green	Tan Suede Green	French Grey Black	French Grey Black
Carmen Red	Red	Red	Red	Black	Black
British Racing Green	Tan Suede Green	Tan Suede Green	Tan Suede Green	Gunmetal Black	Gunmetal Black
Cornish Grey	Red Light Blue Dark Blue Grey	Red Light Blue Dark Blue Grey	Red Light Blue Dark Blue Grey	French Grey Black	French Grey Black

CHASSIS NUMBERS/DATES

Model	Years Manufactured	Chassis Numbers	
		RHD	LHD
Fixed Head Coupé (FHC)	1957–1960	824001	834001
Drophead Coupé (DHC)	1957–1960	827001	837001
Open Two-Seater (OTS)	1958–1960	820001	830001

'DN' suffix indicates fitment of overdrive.

Engine Numbers commence: 3.4, V.1001; 3.8, VA.1001; 3.4 'S', VS.1001; 3.8 'S', VAS.1001.

BUYING GUIDE

Buying an XK is a high risk sport and should only be indulged in after thoroughly acquainting oneself with the subject. The cars are without doubt among the most difficult of all to restore, and the cost and duration of restoration reflects this.

Your first action should be to seek out other enthusiasts who will be able to warn and recommend as a result of their experiences. It is important to learn from their successes and, above all, their mistakes. Sadly the old car world is spiced with plenty of companies which cannot achieve what they purport to offer, through either malice or incompetence. Encouragingly, matters are improving all the time, and today there is a wider selection of real restoration experts than ever before.

If you have the time and ability, or the aptitude and willingness to acquire that ability, there is no substitute for restoring the car yourself. However, it is unlikely that you will be able to carry out all operations – you are bound to need some professional assistance.

The first point I would make is to urge you to go to an XK specialist, unless you want a company to learn on your car. The next point – and equally important – is to choose a firm only after some checking and comparison. Some of the biggest rogues have had the most impressive advertisements. In fact, the chances are that you will not see the real experts advertising extensively because they do not need to seek work.

It is vital to speak to as many specialists as possible and to learn from their comments and advice. Gradually you should be able to weigh up who really knows his subject and who does not. There is no better testamonial than examples of their work and satisfied customers. The length of time they have been in business and carrying out this work is no guarantee, but in most cases it is highly significant.

Some firms will seem ridiculously expensive, others cheap. The cheap ones are unlikely to have been in business very long, or, if they have, it is very likely they will gradually increase the quote as the work progresses until the cost is at least the same as, if not more than, the seemingly expensive firm.

Ideally, you should locate suitable specialists before buying a car, so that when you find a car for sale you will be able to seek their advice. If this is not possible, the rest of this section should hopefully guide you through the minefield!

As the bodywork is by far the most expensive area of the car to restore, it is the section that needs the most careful examination when you buy. Working backwards, you should examine the following areas for corrosion, paint bubbling, welded panels lifting and filler:

Bottoms of front wings
Under headlamp pods
Sidelamp mouldings (other than earlier 120s)
Wing sides
Vent box area (other than earlier 120s)
Wing tops
Wired edges
Battery boxes (when fitted)
Hinge area (try lifting the doors at the open end)
Sills
Doors (particularly at the bottoms)
Shut face area
Rear floor area (on models with occasional rear seats)
Inner rear wings
Side tonneau panels
Rear wings (particularly the area where the three last named panels meet with each other and the wing piping)
Spare wheel tray

It is important that the car is complete mechanically because parts that cannot necessarily be obtained can usually be reconditioned.

Interior trim is probably the hardest area for the amateur to tackle, but fortunately there are several companies specialising in XK trim. Suffolk & Turley actually have the original factory patterns and formerly worked for Jaguar. You would expect the simpler OTS models to be rather cheaper to retrim than the more complex DHC models, but this is not so – the extra OTS cockpit details compensate for its simpler hood.

In spite of the heavy gauge steel used in the construction of the XK chassis, time is catching up with even the most carefully preserved examples, and several areas must be examined. These are the rearmost lengths where the rear spring hanger is situated, the area around the front mounting of the rear spring and the area around the front suspension posts. In recent times these chassis checks have assumed a new importance as it has been known for chassis to be economically unrepairable. Sections can usually be repaired, but check these areas carefully – new chassis are unavailable at the time of writing. Owing to its great strength, it is rare to find a twisted XK chassis. A good guide is to inspect the gap between the chassis members and the torsion bars at the front. If the two are not parallel, any twisting will be seen easily.

As time progresses, more remanufactured exterior trim pieces become available, but some important items still cannot be obtained, other than by a long, tedious and probably fruitless search through autojumble stands. As this is the area that causes professional restorers the most headaches, it would not be sensible to buy a car with missing or damaged exterior trim.

You should be extremely wary of buying a car that purports to have been restored, unless this can be proved to have been done by one of the 'expert' specialists. Many have been done by 'bodgers' or dealers who have a target selling price in mind (and thus a budget) which limits restoration expenditure. Unrestored and part-restored cars can be bought 'in boxes': this may seem a cheaper way to begin, but even an expert would have trouble making sure that everything was there.

My advice is always to buy the worst car you can find and restore it – with a few qualifications. It is vital that certain items of external trim are not missing and can be replated. It is imperative to check that the chassis does not have extensive rot. Ideally the car should have the original engine and be relatively complete, but as far as the body is concerned there is little difference between the dreadful looking car, one that looks shabby and a number of supposedly glamorous examples. Without their paint, the superficially better cars will look just like the dreadful ones; they would therefore cost the same to restore, but would have cost very much more to buy.

One advantage of rising prices is that it is now financially feasible to restore XKs properly. Restoration is an expensive, lengthy and tortuous operation, but if you want an XK to use as it was designed to be used, there is no better way. At the end of the process one will be able to sample the unique joys of XK motoring, whether it be in an XK120, an XK140 or an XK150.

DELIVERIES

Years	Home Sales			Export Sales			
	OTS	FHC	DHC	OTS	FHC	DHC	'S'
1949 (120)				62			
1950	185			1142			
1951	261			1062	187		
1952	67	3		1571	1367		
1953	78	76	141	1160	806	1099	
1954	18	73	122	2010	225	405	
1954 (140)	7	1	2	474	2	68	
1955	35	461	284	1421	1189	1124	
1956	7	270	144	1194	844	1106	
1957		1		212	32	65	
1957 (150)		112	1		856	160	
1958	5/6	513	243	1173	1163/1	781	693
1959	2/40	358	151	107/147	638/92	530/135	
1960	22	216	148	66	475	443	
1961	1	6	6		5		

Regrettably there is confusion over 150 'S' models. The figures after the '/' denote these models and are almost certainly correct. The figure of 693 in the 'S' column is presumed to cover all models. No detail is available with regard to a breakdown of 'S' models in 1960 or '61.

RESTORERS, DEALERS AND PARTS SPECIALISTS

Classic Autos
10 High Street, Kings Langley, Herts
Tel: Kings Langley (09277) 62994
Principal: Aubrey Finburgh
Parts, panel work and restoration.

Classic Dashboards
Tel: Bournemouth (0202) 575167
Principal: Dusty Whibley
Re-lacquering and repair of interior wood trim.

Classic Power Units
Tile Hill, 18 Trevor Close, Coventry
Tel: Coventry (0203) 461136
Principal: George Hodge
XK engine rebuilding specialist.

Contour Autocraft
Station House, French Drove, Gedney Hill, Spalding, Lincs PE12 0NR.
Tel: Holbeach (0406) 330504
Principals: Iain and Bruce Macleod
Manufacturers of panels and complete body assemblies.

Coventry Auto Components
Billingwood, Waste Lane, Berkswell, Coventry, Warwickshire
Tel: Coventry (0203) 464644
Principal: Trevor Scott-Worthington
Specialist in body and interior trim, brake, electrical and suspension parts. Catalogue available.

DK Engineering
Unit D, 200 Rickmansworth Road, Watford, Herts WD1 7JS
Tel: Watford (0923) 55246
Principal: David Cottingham
Sales, parts and restoration.

Alan R. George
Plot 11, Small Firms Compound, Dodwells Bridge Industrial Estate, Hinckley, Leics.
Tel: Hinckley (0455) 615937
Principal: Alan George.
Manual and automatic transmission specialist

Bill Lawrence
9 Badger's Walk, Dibden Purlieu, Hampshire
Tel: Hythe (0703) 846768
Principal: Bill Lawrence
Manufacturers of panels and complete body assemblies.

David Manners
991 Wolverhampton Road, Oldbury, West Midlands B69 4RJ
Tel: Birmingham (021) 544 4040
Principal: David Manners
Suppliers of stainless steel exhausts.

Marina Garage Ltd
7 Woodside Road, Southbourne, Bournemouth
Tel: Bournemouth (0202) 417177
Principal: Bob Davis
Restoration.

RS Panels
Kelsey Close, Attleborough Fields Industrial Estate, Nuneaton CV11 6RS.
Tel: Nuneaton (0203) 388572/89561
Principal: Bob Smith
Manufacturers of wings, restoration, and paintwork.

Suffolk & Turley
Unit 7, Attleborough Fields Industrial Estate, Garrett Street, Nuneaton, Warwickshire
Tel: Nuneaton (0203) 381429
Principals: Eric Suffolk and Mick Turley
Trimming specialists and suppliers of trim kits.

Vintage & Classic International Ltd
Unit 43B, Hartlebury Trading Estate, Kidderminster, Worcs DY10 4JB
Tel: Stourport (0299) 251353
Manufacturers and stockists of Lucas spares.

Pieter Zwakman
C. de Vriesweg 17 Industr. Estate, 1746 CL Dirkshorn, Holland
Tel: 31 2245 848
Principal: Pieter Zwakman
Parts specialist and restoration.